A CONTEMPLATIVE READING OF THE GOSPEL

Matthew

The Journey Toward Hope

By Elena Bosetti

Pauline
BOOKS & MEDIA
Boston

Library of Congress Cataloging-in-Publication Data

Bosetti, Elena.
  [Matteo. English]
  Matthew : the journey toward hope / Elena Bosetti. — 1st English ed.
      p. cm.
  ISBN 0-8198-4848-4 (pbk.)
  1. Bible. N.T. Matthew—Criticism, interpretation, etc. I. Title.
  BS2575.52.B67 2006
  226.2'06—dc22

                                    2006014762

The Scripture quotations taken from the Old Testament and contained herein are from the *New Revised Standard Version Bible: Catholic Edition,* copyright © 1989, 1993, Division of Christian Education of the National Council of the Churches of Christ in the United States of America. Used by permission. All rights reserved.

Texts of the New Testament used in this work are taken from *The New Testament: St. Paul Catholic Edition,* translated by Mark A. Wauck, copyright © 2000 by the Society of St. Paul, Staten Island, New York, and are used by permission. All rights reserved.

Cover design by Rosana Usselmann

Cover art Cover art: Saint Matthew: Gospels of the Cisoing Abbey, mid-twelfth century, France. Bridgeman-Giraudon / Art Resource, NY.

"P" and PAULINE are registered trademarks of the Daughters of St. Paul.

English language edition arranged through the mediation of Eulama Literary Agency

Original edition published in Italian under the title *Matteo. Un cammino di speranza*

Translated by Julia Mary Darrenkamp, FSP

Copyright © 1997 Centro Editoriale Dehoniano, Bologna

First English edition, 2006

Published by Pauline Books & Media, 50 Saint Paul's Avenue, Boston, MA 02130-3491. www.pauline.org.

Printed in the U.S.A.

Pauline Books & Media is the publishing house of the Daughters of St. Paul, an international congregation of women religious serving the Church with the communications media.

1 2 3 4 5 6 7 8 9   11 10 09 08 07 06

To Tino Formigoni,
a wise friend
who built his house on rock

Contents

CHAPTER FOUR
"Blessed are the poor"

Introduction

*D*o you ever read the last page of a book first to find out how the story ends? Well, don't change your reading habits now, because the last page of Matthew holds the key to the entire Gospel. It presents the first encounter of the disciples with the Risen Lord, but also their last.

This solemn scene takes place in Galilee on the mountain that Jesus had pointed out to them. The name of the mountain, however, is not given. This reminds us of earlier important Gospel scenes that have taken place on a mountain: Jesus' victory over the third temptation, the Master's authoritative teaching, and his solitary prayer at night. But besides these occasions, there were also his encounters with the sick—among them the lame and the blind, who would have been healed more easily on a level plain. Then, too, it was on a mountain that Peter, James, and John contemplated the transfigured face of the Master, radiant with glory, which after the resurrection is now shown to the whole group of disciples. They are no longer the Twelve, they are the eleven. Someone is missing from their group who should have been present for this appointment with the Lord. Judas' defection is in fact a reminder that all of the disciples abandoned the Master on the night of his passion. In his great mercy, however, the Lord summons them to the mountain, takes his leave from them again, and sends them to people of every race and culture. The theme of mission is fundamental to the Gospel of Matthew.

Community in mission, in order to build fraternity and the family of God. Announcement and baptism, rebirth and new life, within the current of the eternal love of the Father, of the Son, and of the Holy Spirit. This is a journey toward hope.

In the first chapter, which has an introductory character, we will approach the Gospel of Matthew using an architectural and theological outline. Matthew's Gospel attracts us for various reasons: its clear language, its systematic approach, its awareness of biblical and Jewish roots. Of the three synoptics, Matthew is undoubtedly the most Semitic: he uses parallelisms, inclusions, chiasms—different techniques typical of the Eastern way of communicating. Matthew's Gospel contains the most numerous biblical citations, so many that the Old Testament could rightly be considered its primary source.

In the following chapters we will approach the text directly, highlighting three particular aspects dear to our evangelist: the face of Christ, the Church as a community in mission, and the dimension of ethics. In the foreground undoubtedly shines the face of Christ, whom Matthew presents as Teacher and compassionate Shepherd. He alone reports the unique invitation that Jesus, the Master who is meek and humble of heart, extends: "Come to me, all you grown weary and burdened, and I will refresh you" (11:28).

How did Jesus dream of his community? The Sermon on the Mount gives us the answer, but so does the example of Christ who "comes down" in order to take on our infirmities. The community of disciples must undertake the very same journey as their Master. They cannot close in on themselves, for they are fundamentally missionary; they are sent to give what they have received freely and gratuitously. Matthew does his best to make sure the Church remains faithful to the spirit of the Gospel by being humble and fraternal in all things, by living in benevolence and forgiveness, and by taking care of the little ones and those who are "last," with whom Christ identified himself.

Our evangelist highlights the ethical dimension, perhaps to counter the subtle beginnings of a certain religious formalism. He puts the ecclesial community on its guard against empty rhetoric, spiritualism, and liturgies that do not transform life: "Not everyone who says to me, 'Lord, Lord,' will enter the kingdom of heaven" (7:21). Matthew's ethics are radical, based on love. There is nothing ambiguous about them, however: Jesus is herald of the

Good News, and not simply a teacher of justice! Therefore, not only ethics, but Gospel. A *journey toward hope.*

CHAPTER ONE

"Things new and old"
A Gospel to live

Like a splendid basilica

*I*f you read Matthew after having read Mark, you get the feeling of going from a Romanesque church, with basic architectural lines and scarce decorative elements, to a Byzantine basilica, with great apses, gilded mosaics, and, at the center, the solemn figure of Christ Pantocrator.

On the vestibule wall going into this splendid basilica the symbolic phrase is written: "And they shall give him the name Emmanuel, which is translated 'God-with-us' [*meth'hêmôn*]" (Mt 1:23). It is a promise coming from the past and gathering the hope of Israel (Isa 7:14). In effect, one cannot enter this magnificent basilica—that is, Matthew's story—without hope as the key. Within the basilica's central apse, the phrase returns, finding its fulfillment in the last words of the Risen One to his Church: "Behold, I am with you [*meth'hymôn*]" (28:20).

Ten fulfillment citations

The Gospel of Matthew appears to be "like a work of art, like a well-composed literary product in which multiple meanings are interwoven."[1] Undoubtedly among these is one showing how the Christ-event *fulfills* the promises of God, or rather, the hopes of Israel. One cannot enter into Matthew's account without such hope as the gateway. This is the reason for the many biblical citations that are woven throughout his story: to show that this hope finds its fulfillment in Jesus the Messiah.[2]

Ten citations in particular grab our attention. Each of them is introduced with a typical formula, constructed of the verb *pleròô,* which means "to be fulfilled, to accomplish." The formula usually sounds like this: "this happened *in order to accomplish* [that is, to bring to fulfillment] what the Lord said through means of the prophets."

These passages, called precisely "fulfillment citations," run through Matthew's account like a connecting thread:

---

1. J. Gnilka, *Il Vangelo di Matteo,* 2 vols. (Brescia: Paideia, 1991), II, 759.

2. Matthew contains forty explicit messianic citations and more than one hundred that are implicit. In Mark, there are sixteen explicit and forty implicit; in Luke, there are four explicit (in the account of the temptation) and twenty-six implicit; and in John, there are twenty explicit and forty-two implicit citations. Cf. R. H. Gundry, *The Use of the Old Testament in St. Matthew's Gospel, with Special Reference to the Messianic Hope* (Leiden: Brill, 1967).

Fulfillment citations	Matthew	O.T.
1. Behold, the virgin shall be with child...	1:22–23	Isa 7:14
2. I called my son out of Egypt.	2:15	Hos 11:1
3. A voice was heard in Ramah...	2:17–18	Jer 31:15
4. He shall be called a Nazorean.	2:23	Isa 11:1
5. Land of Zebulon and land of Naphtali...	4:14–16	Isa 9:1–2
6. He took away our illnesses...	8:17	Isa 53:4
7. Behold my servant whom I have chosen...	12:17–21	Isa 42:1–4
8. I will open my mouth in parables...	13:35	Ps 78 (77):2
9. Tell the daughter of Zion...	21:4–5	Isa 62:11
10. And they took the thirty pieces of silver...	27:9b–10	Jer 32:9–10

Characteristic of Matthew, the citations are meant to show that God has given his people the key they need to recognize the Messiah. The priests and scribes of Jerusalem may read these passages of Scripture correctly (cf. 2:5–6), but they are unable to see their fulfillment in Jesus of Nazareth.

Matthew, instead, is "the scribe-become-disciple," who is able to take from the treasure of the Scriptures "both new things and old" (13:52) because he recognizes in Jesus the Emmanuel, the God-with-us (28:20).

Scholars are not lacking who propose that the architecture of the entire Gospel is based on these ten citations.[3] But other elements also emerge and attract our attention as well.

The five discourses

The so-called *discourses* strike us immediately as five majestic columns or sections that gather the words of the Lord into the shape of preaching. Here is the list (the numbers indicate chapters):[4]

— the discourse on the mountain: 5–7;

— the discourse on mission: 10;

— the discourse in parables: 13;

— the discourse on the Church: 18;

— the discourse on the end times: 24–25.

---

3. M. Quesnel, *Jésus Christ selon saint Matthieu: Synthèse théologique* (Paris: Desclee, 1991), 28–30.

4. "The five discourses, which encamp majestically like pillars in the construction of the Gospel of Matthew, not only reveal its precious catechetical dimension—which has remained justifiably predominant in Church use—but also the profound unity. These have come to be openly referred to as the personal teaching of the 'one Master' Jesus (23:8–10) and uphold the whole structure of the Gospel, to which they give a strong cohesion." Cf. M. Laconi and Collaborators, *Vangeli Sinottici e Atti degli Apostoli* (Turin: Elle Di Ci, 1994), 160.

Given our evangelist's tendency to point out connections with ancient revelation, the number of discourses probably alludes to the Pentateuch, the first five books of the Old Testament.

The five discourses are set into the narration like gemstones, illustrating what they are meant to teach. Matthew designed his work by alternating *verba et gesta,* words and actions. The transition from a discursive to a narrative section is indicated through a formula repeated five times, with slightly different wordings: "When Jesus had finished these words..." (7:28; cf. also 11:1; 19:1); "When Jesus finished these parables..." (13:53); "When Jesus had finished all these words..." (26:1).

Seven narrative sections

While there are *five* discourses, there are *seven* (another symbolic number, indicating fullness)[5] narrative sections, two of which are placed one right after the other: the book of Jesus' origins (Mt 1–2) and a kind of introductory *triptych* (also noted in the other two synoptics) comprised of the preaching of the Baptist, the baptism of

---

5. The numerical grouping is a composition technique which rests on the symbolic value of numbers—above all, the numbers three and seven. The genealogy is structured in three meters of fourteen generations each (3 x 7 x 2); the number three is very frequent: three angelic apparitions to Joseph; three temptations (4:1–11); three groups of miracles in chapters 8–9. Matthew, in particular, prefers the number seven: seven spirits who try to enter the house; seven parables; seven loaves of bread; seven fish and seven hampers; forgiving 70 x 7....

Jesus, and the temptation in the desert (3–4). After the Sermon on the Mount (5–7), Matthew presents a series of ten miracles that describe Jesus in solidarity with human suffering (8–9). The discourse on mission (10) is followed by different reactions from the people (11–12); and the discourse on the parables (13) is followed by the great section on the bread, which brings us right to the summit of Peter's confession of Christ and Jesus' transfiguration (14–17).

After the discourse on the Church (18), Jesus leaves Galilee and goes toward the territory of Judea; he begins his journey toward Jerusalem (19–22). The last great discursive section takes place in Jerusalem and includes the eschatological discourse (23–25). This is followed by the most ancient and closely-woven account in the Gospel: the story of the passion and death, the discovery of the empty tomb, the announcements of the resurrection, and the apparitions of the Risen One himself (26–28).

The evangelist tightly links one episode to another, with ties that are temporal, spatial, causal, and also thematic.

Two parallel summaries

We need to bear in mind something that often escapes readers. Matthew didn't assign titles to his Gospel, nor did he divide his account into chapter and verse as we find in the Bible today. The text was just run on, partly to save space. In addition, few had the text within easy reach. The approach to Sacred Scripture came essentially through hearing, involving the ears more than the eyes. Consequently, the sacred author availed himself of various rhetorical and literary techniques to affect the ears and memories of his listeners. Matthew uses several of these. We have already pointed out the conventional phrases that mark the end of the five discourses. Another technique is indicated by a more elaborate phrase, a kind of "summary" of Jesus' activity, which crops up in two strategic points of the story with almost identical sentences: first during the discourse on the mountain (4:23), and then later at the end of the cycle of ten miracles (9:35).

Mt 4:23	*Mt 9:35*
He traveled throughout all Galilee, teaching in their synagogues, proclaiming the good news of the kingdom, and healing every disease and illness among the people.	Then Jesus went around..., teaching in their synagogues, proclaiming the good news of the kingdom, and healing every disease and illness.

These two summaries mark the beginning and end of a large block of unified material. In other words, the repetition of these sentences, technically known as an *inclusion,* signifies that the text that lies between them should be treated as a unit. Its purpose is to illustrate that Jesus' mission consists of two inseparable aspects: teaching and healing.

Here the reader is being advised that the discourse on the mountain (5–7) and the cycle of miracles (8–9) constitute a unity. In fact, they depict on a larger scale what is being said in the summary phrases—that Jesus teaches and heals. *On the mountain* he reveals himself as the Master who speaks with authority ("You have heard it said, but I say to you..."), and *he descends from the mountain* as the Servant and compassionate Shepherd who takes our infirmities upon himself (8:17).

Is it possible through these signals to lay out the whole plan or architecture of the Gospel of Matthew? This intriguing question has involved many students over the last decades. The difficulty of reaching an objectively discernible plan is due to the fact that the interpreter's point of observation and subjectivity also come into play.

For some scholars the alternation between the narrative and discursive elements is evidence of a symmetrical-concentric structure, where the different parts are arranged around a central theme that is key to the whole Gospel: the explanation of the kingdom in parables.

Here is the outline (the numbers again refer to chapters):

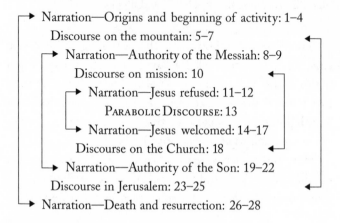

Narration—Origins and beginning of activity: 1–4

Discourse on the mountain: 5–7

Narration—Authority of the Messiah: 8–9

Discourse on mission: 10

Narration—Jesus refused: 11–12

PARABOLIC DISCOURSE: 13

Narration—Jesus welcomed: 14–17

Discourse on the Church: 18

Narration—Authority of the Son: 19–22

Discourse in Jerusalem: 23–25

Narration—Death and resurrection: 26–28

This is a fascinating outline, but one is left with the impression that "holes" exist; in fact, the connections indicated seem rather vague and artificial when confronted with the text.[6] Moreover, it is a static outline, not taking into account other signs conveying the idea of movement and narrative development. Yet it is valuable as regards two temporal pieces of information:

— 4:17: *From then on* Jesus began *to proclaim;*

— 16:21: *From then on* Jesus began *to reveal.*

This formula seems to clearly articulate two progressive phases in Jesus' activity, characterized respectively by the *proclamation* of the Kingdom (4:17–16:20) and the *revelation* of the mystery of the Messiah's suffering, death, and resurrection (16:21–28:20). The first part takes place in Galilee, the second on the journey to Jerusalem.[7]

Here then follows an outline of an architectural plan (once again, the numbers in parentheses correspond to chapters). I like to call it *The Basilica of God-with-us.*

The "book of the genealogy of Jesus the Messiah" makes up the "entrance hall" of this basilica; it anticipates

---

6. This outline was created by J. Caba, *Dai Vangeli al Gesù storico* (Rome: Edizioni Paoline, 1979), 193, which in its turn cites the studies of H. Lohr and of J. C. Fenton. A much more nimble concentric arrangement, which takes into account narrative development, was proposed by H. J. Combrink, "The Structure of the Gospel of Matthew as Narrative," *Tyndale Bulletin* 28 (1983), 34, 61–90.

7. This double temporal caesura allows the narrative structure to be in three parts, as pointed out by J. D. Kingsbury, *Matteo: Un racconto* (Brescia: Queriniana, 1998; original edition: *Matthew As Story* [Philadelphia: Fortress Press], 1988). The narrative character of the first Gospel enjoys noticeable attention among exegetes.

the destiny of Jesus, who was refused by his own people and sought after by the pagans. It also anticipates the same mission for the Church. In fact, there is a certain connection between the arrival of the Magi (2:1–12) and the command to go to all peoples (28:19–20). *The coming* on one hand and *the going* on the other signify two complementary aspects: *attraction and mission.*

Entering the basilica, the five discourses, standing like majestic columns, immediately capture our attention. Eventually our eyes rest on the central apse, where Christ is depicted in all his glory. The eleven prostrate themselves at his feet, in the act of acknowledging him as Lord, as he sends them to all peoples. An inscription runs reassuringly around the image of the Risen One and sums up the entire scene: "Behold, I am with you all days, even to the end of the world."

Introduction
"He will be called Emmanuel, God-with-us"

First part
"From then on Jesus began to preach"
IN GALILEE

The scribe who becomes disciple

What does this well-organized account say for the one who put it together? Matthew does not put his name on the cover, nor does he insist on authors' rights; everything focuses on the words of Jesus. But Matthew can't stop his work from indirectly revealing something of himself and clearly indicating his pastoral concerns. The very harmony he succeeds in creating, by alternating discourse and narrative, seems dictated by pastoral reasons, from a living desire that practice would correspond to doctrine, and that the Gospel listened to would be the Gospel lived!

Perhaps the best "identikit" for Matthew can be taken from a saying of Jesus: "Every scribe who is a disciple of the kingdom of heaven is like a man who is master of a house, who brings from his storeroom both new things and old" (13:52). Yes, Matthew can be seen in this icon of the scribe who searches the Scriptures and finds within them meaning and fulfillment.

Our evangelist remained fascinated by the figure of Jesus Christ, the Emmanuel, the only Master and Shepherd. It was not enough for Matthew to follow Jesus; he also wanted to make him known, drawing from the treasure of the Scriptures "what is new and what is old." And, surprisingly, the new things are better.[8]

After having taken time to appreciate the great architectural lines found in the Gospel of Matthew, I would now like to focus on its theological message—highlighting, in particular, three thematic points: Christ, the Church, and the importance of ethics.

The face of Christ

The authority and majesty of the Risen One who appears at the conclusion of the Gospel of Matthew can-

---

8. Ancient tradition never hesitated in identifying the evangelist with the Apostle Matthew, whose name recurs in every list of the apostles (Mt 10:3; Mk 3:18; Lk 6:15; Acts 2:13). Moreover, the first Gospel identifies Matthew with the tax collector of Capernaum (Mt 9:9), while Mark and Luke speak of Levi, son of Alphaeus (Mk 2:14; Lk 5:27). Beyond these texts there is no mention of Matthew in the whole New Testament. Papias of Hierapolis (A.D. 110–120) speaks of him at the beginning of the second century, affirming that Matthew "put in order sentences (*lòghia*) in the Hebrew dialect, and which each one could therefore interpret as they were able." This testimony was passed on by Eusebius in his *Ecclesiastical History*, III, 39, 6.

not allow us to forget the image of humility and meekness particularly dear to our evangelist. It is enough to think of the invitation that we find only in his Gospel, where Jesus presents himself as the poor one who entrusts himself totally to the Lord: "Come to me, all you grown weary and burdened...learn from me, for I am gentle and humble hearted" (11:28–29).

Son of David and son of Abraham

The Christological perspective, which presents Jesus Christ as the *son of David and the son of Abraham,* is introduced at the end of the first chapter. This is something predominant in the Gospel of Matthew. Jesus fulfills the great messianic expectations through this double sonship, in which we glimpse a certain tension between his partiality (Israel) and universality (all the nations).

As *son of David,* Jesus is the king announced by the prophet (2 Sam 7:12–16). He is both heir of the promises made to the house of David and the Messiah who came from Bethlehem and who leads Israel with the very strength of the Lord (see the oracle of Mic 5:1–4, cited in Mt 2:6). But as *son of Abraham,* Jesus goes beyond the horizons of Israel in order to fulfill that promise of blessing extended to all nations of the earth, the whole human family (cf. Gen 12:3; Gal 3:8).

So right from the very first chapter a tension exists between *partiality* and *universality,* which runs through the entire account. While the body of the Gospel underscores Jesus' *partiality*—the priority of his mission to Israel—the

beginning and end display an open *universality* on his part.
Jesus fulfills the blessing of Abraham for all the nations,
symbolically represented by the Magi who come from the
East to worship him (2:1–11). The scene becomes a kind of
prolepsis or anticipation of what will happen at the story's
end, when the Risen One, in the fullness of his messianic
power, will send his disciples to all nations, to introduce
them into the family of the Holy Trinity (28:19–20).

This takes place precisely at the end of the Gospel,
after the Passover, when we see the face of the Risen One.
But prior to that event, how did Jesus reveal himself?
What awareness of his mission did he have? Only
Matthew mentions Jesus uttering a statement that sounds
a bit restrictive: "I was sent only to the lost sheep of the
house of Israel" (15:24). Jesus' answer to the Canaanite
woman (who obtains the requested grace from "the Son of
David") clearly expresses his awareness of being sent in the
first place to his own people, to reunite and lead Israel as
the new David of whom Ezekiel 34 speaks. However, what
ultimately happens is still more dramatic: Israel does not
welcome him but instead calls down on itself his blood
(27:25).

On the other hand, Matthew never uses the title "son
of David" in the triumphal terms of a political messianism.
Rather, he interprets the title from a perspective of solidarity with the poor, the sick, and the needy—as in 9:27,
where the two blind men cry out: "Have mercy on us, son
of David." They call after Jesus along the road, not reaching him until he arrives at the house to which he was

going, an image that evokes the Church. It is surprising that a foreign woman, the Canaanite mentioned earlier, would also call Jesus by this title (15:22).

Son of the living God

Son of God is another title that doesn't appear at the beginning of the Gospel, but still wonderfully describes who Jesus is for Matthew.

There is no justification for counterposing the two son-ships, since already in 2 Samuel 7:14 God calls the son of David "my son." Even Simon Peter, in his confession of faith at the center of the Gospel, holds together these two aspects of Davidic messianism and divine sonship: "You are the Messiah, the son of the living God" (16:16). Far from contradicting each other, the two titles comprise a whole. From what perspective? From the perspective of integral love, which takes shape in the Servant/Son of God who takes upon himself our infirmities. Not by chance does Matthew cite Isaiah 53:4 at the end of his first group of miracles (8:17) and Isaiah 42:1–4 in another context of healings (12:15–21).[9]

---

9. D. J. Verseput, who has dedicated himself to a precise study of the title "Son of God" in Matthew, holds that the implication of obedience to the Father inclusive in such a title is useful in justifying the humble aspect of the Davidic Messiah: "The Role and Meaning of the 'Son of God' Title in Matthew's Gospel," *New Testament Studies* 33 (1987), 532–556; cf. also: D. Hill, "Son and Servant: An Essay on Matthean Christology," *Journal for the Study of the New Testament* 6 (1980), 2–16; J. D. Kingsbury, "The Title of 'Son of God' in Matthew's Gospel," *Biblical Theology Bulletin* 5 (1975), 3–31.

The only Master and Shepherd

Along with the titles just mentioned—and which we could label "traditional" inasmuch as they appear also in Mark and Luke—only Matthew strongly claims for Jesus the title of *Teacher* or *Master* (23:8–10).

What exactly does this title signify, and what does our evangelist mean when he places it within the five discourses—above all in the first, where Jesus speaks with unheard-of and unthinkable authority for a Jewish rabbi: "You have heard it said, but I say to you"? Such authority comes to be recognized by the crowd, awed by his teaching because, as our evangelist points out, "he was teaching them on his own authority, and not like their scribes" (7:29).

Jesus does not simply teach a doctrine but a way of justice: He is a master of life! He alone is really the Master. The restriction sounds polemical against presumed masters or, as the evangelist defines them, "false prophets" (7:15), but it is also indicative of a community that must always rediscover its constitution, or rather its being a community of brothers and sisters at the feet of the Master: "But don't *you* be called 'Rabbi,' for one is your teacher, and all of you are brothers.... Nor shall you be called teachers, for you have one teacher, the Messiah" (23:8–10).

And this Master has the heart of a shepherd: "When he saw the crowds he was moved with pity for them because they were worried and helpless, like sheep without a shepherd" (9:36). Whether it is the aspect of announcing or the ministry of healing, both of which are explicitly linked in 9:35, what is underscored is the great solidarity of Christ, Master and compassionate Shepherd.[10]

The face of the Church

The term *ekklêsìa,* "church," appears frequently in Paul, but in the Gospels it comes up only three times, and all three instances occur in Matthew. The word first appears in 16:18 and then twice more in 18:17. This lexical fact deserves our attention. In the *Septuagint,* the Greek translation of the Old Testament, seventy-six out of ninety-six times this term is used to translate the Hebrew *qahàl,* that is, the assembly or convocation of the people God has liberated from Egypt and bound to himself with a covenant pact. But what significance does this word contain in Matthew?

After Peter's profession of faith in 16:18, Jesus promises to found on him his *ekklêsìa.* The Church of God becomes the Church of Christ, the messianic community of which everyone can be a part if they, as Peter, recognize in Jesus the Christ, the Son of the living God.[11]

In 18:17 the sense of *ekklêsìa* is different. The context suggests the idea of a local community that comes togeth-

---

10. On the theme of Shepherd in the Gospel of Matthew, see F. Martin, "The Image of the Shepherd in the Gospel of Saint Matthew," *Science and Spirit* 37 (1975), 261–301.

11. The aspect of covenant and the multiple connections between the prologue and the epilogue were especially studied by H. Frankemölle, *Jahwe-Bund und Kirche Christi* (Münster: Aschendorf, 1984).

er in the name of Christ their Lord. The duty entrusted to them is not one of condemning or reproving the sinner, but rather of helping that person to recognize his or her sin in order to find healing and salvation.

A fraternal community

The members of the Church are brothers and sisters,[12] and they are exhorted to behave as such. Jesus himself calls the disciples "my brothers" (28:10). Those who do the will of the Father are considered his new family (12:46–50). And this family of brothers and sisters gathers around the Father with confidence, as Jesus does, and lives this fraternal relationship in terms of acceptance and forgiveness.

There is no doubt that the discourse on the Church in Matthew's Gospel is strongly Christological.[13] To realize the importance of this statement, it is enough to look at the outline of the missionary and ecclesial discourses, both of which highlight a certain correspondence between Jesus and his disciples:

> "Whoever receives you receives me; and whoever receives me receives the one who sent me" (10:40).

---

12. For a thorough examination of the subject: S. Grasso, *Gesù e i suoi fratelli. Contributo allo studio della cristologia e dell'antropologia nel Vangelo di Matteo* (Bologna: EDB, 1994); W. G. Thompson, *Matthew's Advice to a Divided Community. Mt 17:12—18:35* (AnB 44) (Rome: Biblical Institute Press, 1970).

13. On the ecclesiological relevance of the second discourse of Matthew, see M. Grilli, *Comunità e missione: le direttive di Matteo. Indagine esegetica su Mt 9:35—11:1* (Frankfurt am Main: Peter Lang, 1992).

"Whoever receives one such child in my name, receives me" (18:5).

The little ones and the disciples are objects of God's particular protection, which is why we should be careful not to look down on them (18:10–11).

Between Israel and the nations

Like Jesus, so also the Church is closely tied to the story of Israel. "For the first evangelist the 'event' of Jesus becomes paradigmatic in order to resolve the problem of the relationship between Israel and the Church. Therefore Christology is still the key to interpreting the saving story of God in its fundamental stages."[14]

The first criterion for understanding such a relationship is God's fidelity, which is expressed in the dialectic of promise and fulfillment. Jesus brings the salvific plan of God to fulfillment, as the citations of fulfillment in particular demonstrate.

But the biblical story also reveals the people's infidelity, and this second criterion comes into play in the reading of Israel's dramatic refusal. Theirs is not a total and complete refusal, however. A small remnant welcomes Jesus the Messiah and therefore assures the accomplishment of the divine promises. In this sense "the Church is not the 'new' people of God, and neither is it the 'new' Israel, because the people of God is and remains only one: those gathered around Jesus, the Christ and Lord, in whom the

---

14. R. Fabris, *Matteo* (Rome: Borla, 1982), 31.

hopes and promises of Israel come to their complete fulfillment."[15]

Besides, Israel's refusal opens the door to the new economy of salvation for all the nations. Studied in context and applying the synchronic method, the texts show that the theme of universalism—in particular the aspect of a salvation to be shared with the pagan nations—is well organized and gradually developed within the Gospel of Matthew.[16]

Matthew's Church feels itself involved in missionary activity. It recognizes the force of attraction that the words and the life of Jesus exercise on all those who humbly seek salvation and liberation.

Ethical importance

More than any other evangelist, Matthew underlines the ethical aspect: "Not everyone who says to me, 'Lord, Lord,' will enter the kingdom of heaven; no, the one who does the will of my Father in heaven will" (7:21). And "unless your righteousness greatly exceeds that of the scribes and Pharisees, you will never enter into the kingdom of heaven," declares the Master at the beginning of his first discourse (5:20). He himself is the way of absolute justice.

---

15. Fabris, *Matthew*, 32. The ecclesiology theme is fundamentally based on the book by W. Trilling, *Das wahre Israel* (München: St. Benno, 1964), trans. in Italian: *Il vero Israele. Studi sulla teologia del Vangelo de Matteo* (Casale Monferrato: Piemme, 1992); see also G. N. Staton, *A Gospel for a New People: Studies in Matthew* (Edinburgh: T&T Clark, 1992).

16. See, for example, G. Tisera, *Universalism According to the Gospel of Matthew* (Frankfurt am Main: Peter Land, 1993).

But the emphasis on ethics has been the cause of misunderstandings and arguments from the very beginning. This pertains especially to the Sermon on the Mount, where Jesus declares that he has not come to abolish the Law and the Prophets but rather "to fulfill them" (5:17). Unable to accept this statement, Marcion (second century A.D.) did not hesitate to exclude Matthew from the canon of inspired texts, inasmuch as his view opposed Paul's!

Luther resolved the implicit tension in the first Gospel by leading Matthew back to Paul. The radical nature of the Sermon on the Mount would have no other aim than of demonstrating humanity's radical inability to accomplish the Law, the innate sinfulness of the human person, and, consequently, the necessity of opening oneself through faith in order to accept gratuitous salvation.

This problem is also found in modern Protestant exegesis. Liberal theology makes use of Matthew in order to reconstruct the religious message of Jesus, who is presented as the Master of a sublime ethic. But for Matthew, Jesus is not simply a teacher of justice, no matter how sublime; he is the herald of the coming Reign of God!

In the second half of the tenth century, the first Gospel's radical ethic was seen through the mirror of the community. It was the expression of a pastoral plan, a response to problems that Christians of the second or third generation had faced. For example, the sentence "It is not those who say but those who do..." would reflect the image of a community in danger of religious formalism, a danger from which the evangelist intended to rouse it.

How? By reinforcing that beautiful words and prayers do not automatically give one access to the Reign of heaven. The disciples of the Lord must in fact guard against a multiplication of words in their prayer, something the pagans do! Unequivocal signs of recognition are works of charity and the good that is done to the least, with whom Christ identified himself: the foreigner, the poor, the imprisoned, the sick, and those who find themselves in a situation of need or marginalization (25:40–45).

One could therefore suppose that Matthew's editing is not so much motivated by external causes, such as a clash with the Jewish interpretation of the Law, as primarily by an internal crisis of the Christian community.[17] And the "false prophets" whom Jesus condemns at the end of his Sermon on the Mount (7:15–23) could actually be identified with false Christian teachers.[18]

Beyond these hypotheses, however, there is still the challenge—which Matthew puts to every Christian generation—of the unavoidable tension between faith and practice! His three great intertwining themes are Christ, the Church, and the importance of ethics. For Matthew, Christ will not be detached from the Church nor the Church from Christ. Similarly, the announcement of the Gospel cannot take place without ethics, nor can ethics survive without the announcement of the Gospel.

---

17. Trilling, *Das wahre Israel,* 213–214.

18. V. Fusco, "The 'Face' of the Church of Matthew: Methodological Points with Examples from Mt 7:15–23," *Asprenas* 27 (1980), 3–26; see also V. Fusco, *La casa sulla roccia: Temi spirituali di Matteo* (Magnano: Qiqajon-Comunità di Bose, 1994), 38–48.

CHAPTER TWO

"Emmanuel"

The beginnings of Jesus, the Messiah

(Matthew 1–2)

The book of the genealogy of Jesus the Messiah

*I*magine yourself sitting before a fireplace on a winter evening, surrounded by close family members. The occasion is just perfect for reminiscing about old times. Flames from the log fire flicker and create shadowy images on the walls, while your grandfather pulls out the family photo album and begins his story...

Matthew, too, begins his story by flipping through a kind of family album full of names and remembrances. The album's first page displays a great title, which records the protagonist's family tree:

> A record of the lineage of Jesus Christ,
> son of David, son of Abraham (1:1).

Matthew begins his story with a title that recalls Genesis 5:1: "This is the list of the descendants of Adam." Jesus is the new man who takes the place of Adam, though Matthew does not mention this (as compared with Luke 3:38). However, while Adam's descendants are traced with a series of "begots" (where "to beget" means "to transmit one's own image" to the descendant), with Jesus we are dealing with ascendants, as if to say that all of history finds its fulfillment in him. And the story that Matthew focuses on starts with Abraham, the father of believers.

After the genealogy, which forms a complete whole with the title (1:1–17), five stories follow, as a kind of "mini-Pentateuch" on the origins of Christ:

1. The birth of Jesus: 1:18–25
2. The adoration of the Magi: 2:1–10
3. The flight into Egypt: 2:13–15
4. The massacre of the children of Bethlehem: 2:16–18
5. The return to Nazareth: 2:19–23

Matthew uses the technique of interlaying two happenings—Joseph's cycle of dreams (A) and those of the Magi and of Herod (B)—which probably originally belonged to an independent tradition as far as style and content are concerned. Interweaving the two traditions, our evangelist reveals his own point of view. Neither Joseph nor the Magi nor Herod are the important characters here (even if they could have been so originally in their respective traditions); instead, Jesus alone plays a part in all the stories.[1]

---

1. Cf. H. Boers, *Who Was Jesus? The Historical Jesus and the Synoptic Gospels* (New York: Harper and Row, 1989), 11ff.

These accounts share a fundamental characteristic, "re-reading" traditions about Jesus' origins in light of the ful-fillment of Scripture, a point to which the evangelist and his community are particularly sensitive. For example, Joseph's dreams all finish with a biblical citation that uses the same formula: "this happened so that the Scriptures would be fulfilled."[2]

Here is a comprehensive outline of this splendid book, which tells the *Birth of Jesus according to Matthew*, antici-pating in a nutshell the entire Gospel and its drama:

The Family Tree: 1:1–17

A1. An Angel appears in a dream to Joseph:
     = the announcement of the divine maternity of Mary:
     1:18–25

    B1. The visit of the Magi—the anxiety of Herod:
    2:1–12

A2. An angel appears in a dream to Joseph
     = the announcement of the flight into Egypt: 2:13–15

    B2. The deception of the Magi; Herod orders the
    massacre of the children in Bethlehem: 2:16–18

A3. An angel appears in a dream to Joseph
     = the announcement of the return from Egypt:
     2:19–23.

---

2. On the purpose of these citations, one could make use of: G. M. Soares Prabhu, *The Formula Quotations in the Infancy Narrative of Matthew* (AnB 63) (Rome: Biblical Institute Press, 1976); Stanton, *A Gospel for a New People;* M. Trimaille, "Citations d'acomplissement et architecture de l'Evangile selon S. Matthieu," *Estudios Bíblicos* 48 (1990), 47–79.

After considering this panoramic view, we would do well to pause and look at certain details, beginning with the genealogical tree.

An intricate genealogical tree

Matthew's account opens with a long sequence of names—some famous, most unknown, and almost all of them masculine. The list of Christ's ancestors is compiled in strict fashion, with fixed repetitions and a hammering of the verb "to generate": Abraham begot Isaac; Isaac begot Jacob, and so on. Hearing the list recited, it's hard not to grow bored or sleepy, especially if the reading takes place in a liturgical setting. We might not even be aware of certain variations, such as the double mention of "brothers" ("Jacob fathered Judah and his brothers"; "Josiah fathered Jechoniah and his brothers": verses 2 and 11), and above all the surprising "intrusion" of four feminine names in a list dominated by males. These four women certainly did not excel in holiness or purity of morals, and they were *foreigners* on top of that: Tamar, Rahab, Ruth, and Bathsheba, the wife of Uriah the Hittite.

Foreigners and transgressors, but chosen beforehand by God

If Matthew, unlike Luke who does not mention any women, decided to violate the literary rules of genealogy, he must have had his own good reasons for doing so. But why include women who were foreigners and transgressors, rather than holy and submissive women, according to the canons of feminine virtues appreciated by men? The evangelist does not give us the satisfaction of knowing his reasons, but he does leave us something to help us explore them. And if we take time to investigate the stories behind the names, our initial boredom can give way to wonder as we realize that the God of Scripture reserves the right to undermine plans and upset traditional standards—even ethical ones.[3] If we were to measure these women against conventional ethical parameters (Jewish and Christian), they would be branded with infamy: incest, prostitution, and various intrigues. Definitely fascinating, this genealogical tree that legitimizes the Davidic lineage of Christ, the son of Mary!

And yet, these cunning and often devious women, who made use of all their feminine wiles to gain a heritage, are blessed and chosen by God as ancestors of him who will declare that he has come not to call the just, but sinners (9:13).

Tamar is the bold Canaanite whom the patriarch Judah recognized as "more just" than himself. She remained a childless widow and waited in vain for her father-in-law to fulfill his duty toward her with regard to the Law. Probably fearful after the death of his first two sons, Judah cheated the third, postponing his wedding to his brother's widow and forcing Tamar to return to her father's house. But the woman did not resign herself to her fate; she shrewdly

---

3. For deeper study, I suggest my book: *Donne nel popolo di Dio* (Leumann: Elle Di Ci, 1998), in particular: "Le donne della genealogia di Gesù: ovvero la memoria del grembo materno," 81–88.

obtained what she had been unjustly denied. Veiled as a
prostitute, Tamar waited for her father-in-law at the gates
of Enaim and dealt with him cleverly: "What will you give
me, that you may come in to me?" Judah promised a kid
from his flock, but she immediately asked for a pledge:
"Your signet and your cord, and the staff that is in your
hand" (Gen 38:18). These would be her credentials when
Judah, learning that she was pregnant, would condemn her
to death: "Bring her out, and let her be burned" (Gen
38:24). Denied every juridical authority, Tamar won by
sending the possessions back to her father-in-law with the
message: "It was the owner of these who made me pregnant." And Judah then recognized her moral superiority.
Tamar had won!

Rahab, the generous prostitute of Jericho, risked her
own life to protect the spies sent by Joshua. In exchange,
she asked only for protection for herself and her family
when the city would be turned over to the Israelites.[4] She
was capable of reading a situation, which today we would
call *the signs of the times:* "I know that the Lord has given
you the land" (Josh 2:9). For this she is remembered in
Hebrews 11:31 as a woman of faith: "By faith Rahab the
prostitute did not perish with those who were disobedient,
because she had received the spies in peace." She demonstrates a faith that expresses itself in concrete works, as the
Letter of James reminds us, and that risks the courage of
hospitality: "Likewise, was not Rahab the prostitute also

---

4. The story of Rahab is told in Josh 2:1ff. and 6:22–25.

shown to be righteous by her works when she took the messengers in and sent them out by a different way?" (Jm 2:25)

The third woman is Ruth the Moabite, who was also a widow and childless like Tamar, but who was ready to leave everything behind in order to follow her afflicted mother-in-law, Naomi, and even Naomi's God: "Do not press me to leave you or to turn back from following you! Where you go, I will go; where you lodge, I will lodge; your people shall be my people, and your God my God" (Ruth 1:16). This young foreigner proved herself capable of risking like Abraham; but she also allowed herself to be guided by the wisdom of Naomi, who brought her to an appreciation of her feminine power in order to conquer Boaz and thereby gain a heritage for her deceased husband. The congratulations that the people of Bethlehem extended to Boaz on the day of his wedding connected this woman to the mothers of Israel: "May the LORD make the woman who is coming into your house like Rachel and Leah, who together built up the house of Israel. ...And through the children that the LORD will give you by this young woman, may your house be like the house of Perez, whom Tamar bore to Judah" (Ruth 4:11–12). Never in the entire Bible has so great a blessing been addressed to a foreigner. Ruth, the great-grandmother of David, was likened to the matriarchs of Israel!

Directly connected to David is, above all, the fourth woman, Bathsheba, whom Matthew makes a point of not calling by name: "David fathered Solomon by Uriah's wife." Thus the mother of the heir to the throne is also presented as a stranger inasmuch as she had been the wife of a Hittite.[5]

Although Bathsheba's name is associated with the sin of David, in reality the element that unites these four female ancestors of Christ is not so much *sin* as their *being foreigners.* In the house of David, and therefore in the veins of the Messiah of Israel, there flows also the blood of the non-Hebrew, the blood of the foreign nations represented by these ancestors.

The result is a theological idea of universal openness. Christ's house is open to the pagans not only at the end of the story, with the Risen One's explicit missionary mandate, but right from the beginning, in its very structure and in its supporting columns—the women.

In the construction of this house, Tamar, the Canaanite, enters so to speak at the foundational level; she is co-heir of the benediction that the patriarch Jacob kept apart for Judah: "The scepter shall not depart from Judah, nor the ruler's staff from between his feet, until tribute comes to him; and the obedience of the peoples is his" (Gen 49:10).

Rahab, the prostitute of Jericho, inserts herself in a moment of particular importance, when the Hebrew people enter the Promised Land. Her house will not be eliminated, but remains "in the midst of Israel"—a presence undoubtedly ironic and provoking, but no less prophetic.

---

5. For the story of Bathsheba, see 2 Sam 11:1—12:25.

In fact, while by divine ordinance Israel is under vow to exterminate everything it encounters on its way—a kind of scorched earth in defense of racial and religious purity—a prudent and wise prostitute from Jericho bows to the same divine rule because "she has lived in Israel ever since" (Josh 6:25).

As for Ruth and Bathsheba, they participate firsthand in the construction of the house of David, respectively as ancestress and wife of the ideal king. They are therefore connected with the covenant (*berìt*) that the Lord makes with his descendents forever.

The most longed-for maternity

Let us now return to the list of forefathers, which opens with Abraham (without naming who fathered him) and concludes with the birth of Jesus (without, once again, naming who fathered him):

> Jacob begot Joseph the husband of Mary, of whom was born Jesus, who is called the Messiah. (1:16)

This is a decisive variation, which merits our full attention. In fact, after hearing the incessant "fathered" (*egènnêsen*) repeated thirty-nine times, here is a surprising ending with a passive verb: "was born" (*egennêthê*). Scholars call this a "theological passive"; here it attests to the divine maternity of Mary. It is not Joseph but God himself who is at the origins of the Christ.

At the end of the genealogical family tree, we are told of the human-divine origin of Jesus the Messiah. Taking nothing away from the profundity of the human generations, something is revealed that goes beyond them. The journey started by the believer Abraham effectively reaches what was unhoped for: God himself enters once and for always into humanity's history. "But when the fullness of time had come, God sent forth his Son, born of a woman" (Gal 4:4). It is the faith of Paul and of Matthew, of the first Christians, and of we ourselves.

14 x 3: math or symbolism?

Matthew closes the genealogy with an annotation that has troubled scholars:

> So all the generations from Abraham up to David were fourteen generations, and from David up to the Babylonian Exile were fourteen generations, and from the Babylonian Exile up to the Messiah were fourteen generations. (1:17)

The chain that goes from father Abraham to the son of Mary is therefore articulated in three sections, each comprising fourteen generations. The evangelist is careful to be accurate, though the math does not work out evenly in the last section, where the verb "to generate, to beget" happens only thirteen times (twelve are active verbs and the thirteenth is passive). But this very inconsistency serves as a sign that the numbers are perhaps more symbolic than mathematical.

If the perspective is symbolic, then it remains open to various hypotheses. And in reality, different interpretations have been given to these fourteen refrains times three. Three times fourteen is like saying six times seven, where seven could allude to the divine perfection and six to the incompleteness of man himself. Thus the six-times-seven of human history would reach its perfection in Christ, the firstborn of the new generation.

Then there are those who see in the threefold temporal division the consonants that in Hebrew form the name of David, whose equivalent number is 14 (*dwd:* d=4, w=6, d=4). This symbolism would confirm the royal messiahship of the Christ.

Be that as it may, the number fourteen, which is two times seven, is the symbol of perfection; moreover, multiplied by three, it indicates the sum of perfection, the fullness of time, and the fulfillment of the promises.

Joseph: the dreams and the obedient listener

In Jesus' family album one is often impressed by the importance of the figure of Joseph, the just man, who experiences all the darkness and anguish of the night, yet who nevertheless knows how to dream in preparing for the new day of the Messiah.

Unlike Luke, who in his first two chapters concentrates on Mary while naming Joseph only three times,[6] Matthew mentions him seven times in all. Already this numerical indication—a symbol of fullness—signifies the great spotlight our evangelist puts on this man of faith who is capa-

---

6. The first time was to say that the Virgin Mary was the promised spouse of a man of the house of David, whose name was Joseph (Lk 1:26); the second was in the context of the census (Lk 2:4); and the third was in the scene of the manger and the shepherds: "They went to Bethlehem... and found Mary and Joseph and the baby lying in a manger" (Lk 2:16).

ble of listening. Joseph's obedience recalls that of Abraham (cf. Gen 12:4; 22:3); it is a faith that brings to fulfillment the word announced by the prophets. Not by chance do the three accounts with Joseph as protagonist end with the "citation of fulfillment," that is, with a biblical text that the evangelist declares *fulfilled*, or rather fully realized, in Jesus (1:22; 2:15; 2:23).

And so, there is a fundamental resemblance to Abraham, the father of our faith. But there is something else. A symbolic thread connects the adoptive father of Jesus with the biblical Joseph, the dreamer. Like his namesake, our Joseph is also "a dreamer." The angel of the Lord always appears to him at night, when the mind slumbers. And the dream is the bearer of a message, of a heavenly will that Joseph punctually carries out in silence.

The connection between these two great people is already introduced in the genealogy, where it reads: "Jacob fathered Joseph" (1:16). Those familiar with Scripture will recognize the allusion: just as the patriarch, Jacob, and his son Joseph were a sign of the beginnings of Israel and of its history as a people in Egypt, so this Joseph, also a son of Jacob, recalls a new and surprising beginning of the story of the people of God. Matthew introduces him through two relationships:

— he is the son of Jacob;
— he is the husband of Mary, from whom was born Jesus who is called Christ.

The first relationship speaks of an identity received at birth. Joseph is "the son of," the fruit of, his father. The second, instead, describes an acquired identity, the fruit of freedom. Based on his own choice and decision, Joseph is the spouse, the husband of Mary. This is a strong affective and legal connection that will also socially determine the rest of his life.

The son of Jacob

Let's look at the first relationship. Is it simply a coincidence that Joseph is the son of Jacob? It is hard to evade the compelling effects of this combination of names. The biblical Joseph was the favored son of the patriarch Jacob because he was born of the beautiful but previously sterile Rachel, Jacob's beloved wife. It was precisely the father's boundless affection for this son that engendered the hatred of Joseph's brothers. They waited for the opportune moment to kill him, but then limited themselves to selling him to slave traders who brought him to Egypt.

Is it merely by chance that our Joseph receives the command to go down into Egypt? Just as Joseph the son of Jacob proved to be the instrument of God's providence for his brothers, who went down to Egypt when forced by famine, so our Joseph shows himself to be the instrument of providence with regard to Mary and the infant Jesus (2:13–15).

Already in this initial presentation there is a certain correspondence that goes beyond names or the interweaving of biblical traditions concerning the stories of the patriarchs. This is not a matter of forcing comparisons. Matthew's intention is not to show that Joseph the husband of Mary follows the biblical patriarch in absolutely every respect. Each human story is unrepeatable. The intention here is something else entirely. We are at a crucial point of the story, which for many reasons recalls the beginnings and transcends them. We must wait for a determined crossroads in the historical course of human generations through which the divine plan of salvation is made manifest. Joseph is a witness of a new generation, one which sees heaven descend to earth.

The spouse of Mary

Now let's proceed along the other trail, allowing ourselves to be guided by Matthew's resounding presentation of the spousal relationship of Joseph with Mary, and the birth of a son that involves her and not him.

How can we characterize Joseph's situation in this regard? The text presents him thus: "Joseph the husband of Mary, who gave birth to Jesus, who is called Messiah" (1:16).

There is some similarity here with the story of the women mentioned in the genealogy. In fact, we see a pattern that repeats itself: A fathers B from C:

— Judah fathered Perez and Zerah by Tamar (1:3);

— Salmon fathered Boaz by Rahab (1:5);

— Boaz fathered Obed by Ruth (1:5);

— David fathered Solomon by Uriah's wife (1:6);

— Jacob fathered Joseph the husband of Mary, *who gave birth to* Jesus, who is called Messiah.

One can see a difference, however. Joseph did not "father" a son by Mary, as David did with the wife of Uriah, or Boaz with Ruth, or Judah with Tamar. Mary conceived through the work of another, and not by human means.

Matthew follows the same pattern four times, mentioning alongside the father the name of the mother, and then the son who is particularly important in the line of descendents. According to Jewish hope, the Messiah would come from Judah, designated by Jacob as the bearer of blessing. And this was realized precisely thanks to Tamar, the woman who resorted to the stratagem of incest with her father-in-law in order to guarantee a legitimate descendent. The same goes for the other women: Rahab, Ruth, and Bathsheba.

And so the maternities recorded by Matthew fall under the category of highly irregular situations. Yet it was through these irregular maternities that the divine plan was unexpectedly made manifest. Matthew is careful, however, to specify that the maternity in question is not simply "irregular"; it is on another level entirely. Joseph is not the husband of a child-bride; he is not merely a good man who covers over a mistake made by his fiancée. Joseph is a just man whom God calls to be the father of a son generated by the Holy Spirit.

An unforgettable triptych

From a literary perspective one could speak of a "Joseph triptych," with a series of three connecting stories serving as panels. The first has for its subject the announcement of

Mary's divine maternity; the second, the flight into Egypt; and the third, their return to the land of Israel.

An identical structure accompanies these three panels:

1. An angel appears in a dream bearing a message.
2. Joseph follows the order received.
3. The evangelist finishes with a biblical citation by way of commentary: *"All this took place to fulfill what had been spoken by the prophets."*

The triptych or cycle of stories, however, is not in exact sequence. Here Matthew is playing with literary style. In fact, we find two other accounts placed right in the middle: the visit of the Magi from the East and the massacre of the infants in Bethlehem by order of Herod. Let's stop and take a look at these three panels, which depict the figure of Joseph along the lines of the ancient patriarchs:

— as Abraham (1:18–25);
— as Joseph in Egypt (2:13–15);
— as Moses (2:19–23).

Although he is presented in the genealogy as "the son of Jacob," Joseph of Nazareth conducts himself above all in the manner of Abraham. Unlike the patriarch Jacob, Joseph does not bargain with God; he does not argue or ask for signs or guarantees.[7] He is more like Abraham, who never objected to the word of the Lord but listened and followed. Abraham is the man of obedience; he reacts

---

7. Jacob does this in Gen 28:20–21, where he transforms the divine promise into a bet. See E. Bosetti, *La tenda e il bastone: Figure e simboli della pastorale biblica* (Milan: Edizioni Paoline, 1992), 23–24.

in silence and his actions speak louder than his words. Our Joseph is exactly the same. He never utters a word, whether at the first appearance of the angel or at the second or third appearances.

Joseph asks for not one word of explanation. The doubts that afflict him (should he put her aside? send her away in secret? cf. 1:19) are placed in the hands of the One who is greater and who directs the story. Joseph entrusts himself totally to God. In this he really is similar to Abraham, whom the word of God sends on a journey (Gen 12:4)—a journey that unfolds all uphill. Joseph is a man *who goes beyond—above all, beyond legal interpretation.* He does not stop at what the Law dictates, but exceeds it with a "greater justice" (5:20): his love for Mary. The evangelist recounts that Joseph, the just man, does not want to divorce her as the Law prescribes, but decides instead to put her away secretly. Therefore he goes beyond legal requirements even before the angel appears to him, giving credit to his love for Mary.

But Joseph, a true descendent of Abraham, *goes even further,* entrusting himself to the word of God: "Do not be afraid to take your wife Mary..."(1:20), announces the angel, and Joseph "did as the angel of the Lord had commanded him and took his wife into his house" (1:24). In this uphill journey guided by the word of God that speaks to him in the night, in the depths of his mind plagued with doubt but ready to respond to the ethical questions of what he must do in a concrete situation, Joseph experiences the presence of God-with-us, the Emmanuel.

In the second panel of our triptych, the figure of Joseph is connected to his namesake. He is seen on a journey in a spatial sense: "'Get up, take the child and its mother and flee to Egypt and stay there until I tell you—Herod is going to search for the child to kill it.' So Joseph got up and took the child and its mother and departed by night for Egypt" (2:13–14).

By night. I am struck by this phrase in particular. To dream of an angel during the night seems fairly reasonable. But to get up and leave by night, even for a Bedouin familiar with the desert roads, definitely is not. Even more so, if one considers traveling to a strange country. This detail transcends mere facts and allows us to understand Joseph's state of soul: for him it is also a psychological night. Joseph is not simply a dreamer. He is a man who goes forward in the darkness of faith: "If you try my heart, if you visit me by night, if you test me, you will find no wickedness in me" (Ps 17:3). His rising at night recalls an attitude of prayer: "O LORD, God of my salvation, when, at night, I cry out in your presence, let my prayer come before you" (Ps 88:1–2). He entrusts himself to God who listens to the prayer of the afflicted, and God opens a way for him in Egypt.

The traditional land of oppression then becomes a place of hospitality, a land of welcome. Matthew does not forget the positive role Egypt played as a place of refuge for Abraham (Gen 12:10–20), for Jacob and his sons (Gen 46:1–27), for Jeremiah, and for other political refugees.

In the triptych's third panel we see Mary's spouse also take on a resemblance to Moses, who led Israel out of Egypt: "Get up, take the child and its mother and go to the land of Israel—those who sought the child's life are dead" (2:20). And once more Joseph the dreamer rises, takes the child and his mother, and sets off on a journey. But this time the passage doesn't specify that it was night, because the return journey to their homeland resembles the dawning of a new day.

We have before us a new Joseph, son of Jacob, who saves his family. Are we dealing here with history? Myth? Perhaps more likely *midrash,* that is, a commentary on events within the great biblical perspective, following the evocative force of the fathers of Israel. Joseph serves as a prominent figure at a time when the father's role seems to be in crisis. His is a paternity that transcends biological facts, but cannot be relegated merely to the legal sphere of *hypothetical father.* As caretaker and formator, he models fatherhood as welcome, respect, and concern toward overall development. It is not insignificant that at Nazareth, Jesus was known as the son of Joseph. From him Jesus learned a trade, just as the sons of Zebedee learned from their father how to be fishermen. To everyone Jesus was "the carpenter's son" (13:55).

In conclusion, Joseph of Nazareth, the dreamer, is the man of exodus, who opens the way in the night, entrusting himself totally to God. He is the model of what every true believer in the Church should be.

The Magi, Herod, and the star

Two accounts, which have the Magi and Herod as protagonists, are inserted within Joseph's cycle of dreams. The newborn Messiah is recognized and adored from afar by the Magi, but feared and persecuted by those near him, by Herod and the holy city.

The drama's leitmotif involves a tension between Jerusalem, the questioning city, and Bethlehem, city of the answer. The tension unfolds within six small scenes that are interconnected in groupings of three:

- The initial question is posed by the Magi, who have arrived in Jerusalem following the star (2:1–2), to Herod and his priests and scribes; the question is answered by the Scriptures (2:3–6); the Magi are asked by Herod to return with the answer (2:7–8).

- The Magi journey to Bethlehem following the star (2:9–10); they encounter the baby and Mary his mother, then adore him and offer gifts (2:11); having been warned in a dream not to return to Herod (2:12), the Magi return by another route.

The narrative proceeds like a suspense story. Beginning with the phrase "When Jesus was born in Bethlehem of Judea in the days of King Herod," Matthew immediately gives the reader essential information, while he or she is left ignorant of the Magi and other important players in the story. The reader thus concentrates on how the various protagonists act based on their respective attitudes toward the baby. However, Matthew creates the kind of tension found in a mystery novel: they don't know what we know.

"Where is the newborn king of the Jews?" the Magi ask (2:2). And by asking *where,* they announce that *he is born.* The Good News comes from afar. They have seen his star in the great eastern sky, and like Abraham they have set out on a journey right to the holy city, the first fruits of that pilgrimage of people announced by the prophet:

A multitude of camels shall cover you, the young camels of Midian and Ephah; all those from Sheba shall come. They shall bring gold and frankincense, and shall proclaim the praise of the LORD (Isa 60:6).

A tragic paradox ensues. Instead of producing joy and feasting, the news of the birth of the King causes anguish and agitation in Jerusalem. Not only Herod but the entire city is disturbed. The account dramatically anticipates the story of the passion.

But why this stop in Jerusalem? Why didn't the star lead the Magi directly to their destination? After so long a journey, why didn't they go the rest of the way, less than ten more miles? The star studied by the Magi confirms that he is born, but the where and the why are revealed only by Scripture:

But you, O Bethlehem of Ephrathah, who are one of the little clans of Judah, from you shall come forth for me one who is to rule in Israel, whose origin is from of old, from ancient days (Mi 5:2).

Jerusalem, the city in which the question is asked—by the Magi to Herod and the scribes—offers the correct response through the Scriptures: it is from Bethlehem that the Messiah will shepherd Israel with the strength of

YHWH. His origins descend from King David. The citation in the fifth chapter of Micah offers a complete constellation of thematic images and words: shepherd, people, son of David, king of the Jews....

The artfully-constructed story deftly plays with the fact that the two cities are linked to the name of David. Jerusalem knows, but doesn't move; the scholars of the Book do not budge an inch toward the Shepherd-Messiah. It is not the children of David who go looking for the newborn "king of the Jews," but foreigners. Beneath the cross it will be a Roman centurion who recognizes him; here at his birth it is the Magi who do so. They follow the star of the Messiah ("his star"), which was already foreseen by the pagan prophet Balaam: "A star shall come out of Jacob, and a scepter shall rise out of Israel" (Num 24:17).

The evocative figure of the Magi recalls that of Abraham, father of believers, who gazed enraptured at the stars and tried to count them (Gen 15:5). It is not as if the Magi are trying to name the comet-like star, but they want to understand the symbolic language of this account, which confirms an implicit connection between natural and biblical revelation. These are two ways destined to meet, two matching books that lead to Christ, and the first is interpreted with the help of the second. One does not arrive at the crib of the Messiah without observing creation and without the Scriptures.

The journey of the Magi, therefore, seems to articulate an obligatory course provided by the pagans for the

Church. No one arrives at Bethlehem with only the star as guide, or rather, merely with the light of natural revelation: of creation and of human intelligence. God certainly speaks in many ways, even through the stars (cf. Rom 1:19–20). But one cannot arrive at Bethlehem by skipping over Jerusalem, or rather, without taking into account what the Scriptures say. The star—in the heavens and in one's heart—confirms that the Messiah is born, but where and why are revealed by the prophets.

Yet paradoxically it is not enough to have the Scriptures and to know what they say. This is certainly indispensable for arriving at Bethlehem, but the priests and the scribes did not go off looking for him. The Magi, instead, discovered where to find the baby and arrived full of joy at their destination: "When they entered the house they saw the child with its mother, Mary. They fell on their knees and worshiped him" (2:11).[8]

---

8. The gifts of the Magi—gold, frankincense, and myrrh—have always been interpreted in a symbolic sense, with reference to the humanity and divinity of Christ. A good example of this is found in the passage of St. Ephrem of Syria: "And they opened up their treasures and offered him gifts of gold for his human nature; myrrh, as a figure of his death; and incense to his divinity (Mt 2:11). That is: gold, as to a king; incense, as to God; myrrh, as to him who would be embalmed. Or better still: gold, because they adore him, as adoration is given to one's master; myrrh and incense to indicate the medicine that will heal the wound of Adam" (Ephrem, *Diatessaron,* II, 5, 25; cf. *I Padri vivi. Commenti patristici al Vangelo domenicale: Solennità e feste,* texts chosen by M. Starowieyski, liturgical introductions by J. Miazek [Rome: Città Nouva Editrice, 1982]), 69–71.

The massacre of the children and Rachel's tears

The second account connected to the Magi and Herod points out how the life of Christ was threatened right from his birth, as was that of Moses and Israel. Herod prolongs the role of the oppressive Pharaoh who, devoured by his fear of losing the throne, ordered the killing of the Hebrew children (cf. Ex 2:8–22).

Like Joseph, the Magi are warned in a dream not to go back to Herod to tell him where the baby is, as he had maliciously requested. When he sees that he has been tricked, the king orders the massacre of "all the boys in Bethlehem and all its neighborhood who were two years old or younger, based on the time he had ascertained from the wise men" (2:16).

It is a horrifying decision, based on the logic of tyrannical power exercised throughout the centuries. Herod trembles at the smallest sign of threat, tied in this case to messianic hope. And so, like pharaoh before him, Herod resorts to the most radical solution possible: the killing of the innocents.

We see here the logic of power pitted against messianic hope. First Herod, then the religious heads of Jerusalem, will bring not only the infants but also the entire people to destruction. The evangelist suggests the following text, interpreting the massacre of the children of Bethlehem in light of the prophet Jeremiah:

> Then what was declared by Jeremiah the prophet was fulfilled, when he said,

"A voice was heard in Ramah,
wailing and great mourning;
Rachel weeping for her children,
and she would not be comforted,
because they are no more" (2:17ff.; cf. Jer 31:15).

With powerful imagination Jeremiah describes Rachel, the beloved wife of Jacob, swept up in terrible and inconsolable weeping. At the top of her voice the matriarch cries, "Bury me along the way to Ephrath, that is, Bethlehem" (Gen 35:19), because she sees her sons passing on this road into exile. To go into exile is like dying. No words are capable of comforting the heart of this mother.

I am also struck by the connection Matthew suggests between mothers and their children. Is there any greater sorrow than for a mother to see her children killed? These babies are sacrificed without anyone knowing the reason why, and they—the mothers—continue to live despite the fact that their hearts have died.

Because of this they are connected with the great lament of the mother of their people. Rachel herself cries over the killing of these innocents, the children of Bethlehem who were murdered by the rage of the powerful. She stands for all mothers who in every part of the world continue to cry for their murdered sons and daughters.

The play of names

I would now like to call your attention to a kind of name play that extends across the book of the origins of

Jesus the Messiah, referring not only to *son of David and of Abraham,* but also to *Emmanuel, the Nazarene and/or Nazorean.*

In the first apparition, the angel entrusts to Joseph the duty of naming the *son of Mary;* he is to call him "Jesus," something Joseph promptly does. And by way of explanation Matthew adds: "because he will save his people from their sins" (1:22).

But here, between the order and its execution, he inserts a second name that also receives an explanation: "and they shall give him the name Emmanuel, which is translated, 'God-with-us'" (1:23).

Looking further, we see a third name, connected with Joseph's final dream: "So, having been warned in a dream, he departed for the district of Galilee, and he went and settled in a town called Nazareth to fulfill what was said by the prophets, *'He shall be called a Nazorean'*" (2:22–23). For this final name no explanation is given.

A dynamic is being set in motion here that is not without tension. It runs throughout the entire account as a kind of *play on names,* situated between the present and the future, between prophecy and fulfillment.

Here is an outline that helps to put everything together:

> *and you shall name him* JESUS (1:21)
>   *and they shall give him the name* EMMANUEL (1:23)
> *and he gave him the name* JESUS (1:25)
>   *he shall be called the* NAZARENE/NAZOREAN (2:23)

Why this tension between history and prophecy, between the past and the future ("he is called"/"he will be called")? How do these names play out with their respective meanings, and what do they add to the initial presentation? The genealogical tree ends, in fact, by affirming that of Mary "was born Jesus, called the Christ," or rather, the Messiah (1:16).

But by whom was Jesus called "the Christ"? Only by believers, or also—with a certain irony and contempt—by those who saw in him the disappointment of their own messianic expectations, which differed from those promised by Jesus. The passion account confirms this view. Twice will Pilate, in front of the people who are asking for Jesus' death, use the same expression: "Jesus, who is called the Christ" (cf. 27:17, 22).

Therefore, this name play involves and engages us right to the end of the story, where the last words of the Risen One—"*I am with you*" (28:20)—remind us of the first biblical citation: "He will be called Emmanuel, which means *God-with-us*" (cf. 1:23).

He who saves from sin

The Gospel reader knows from the beginning who Jesus is and what exactly his mission was, but the people of history—his followers and his opponents—didn't know. And so another narrative tension is produced, which runs through the whole Gospel.

In reality, the explanation that Matthew (and only he among the other evangelists) offers for the name of Jesus—"he who saves from sin"—is not too obvious. Literally, Jesus (in Hebrew *Yeshua*) means "YHWH saves."

But saves from what? From famine, from enemies, from sins? It is not specified. This beginning, therefore, is open to different interpretations.

Jesus bears the name of the great leader, Joshua (both names are translated the same way in Hebrew), who brought the people into the Promised Land. In that case the name obviously alludes to salvation as liberation and victory over one's enemies. Matthew, instead, is careful to immediately point out that the salvation tied to Jesus' name is of another kind: it is liberation from sin. *Nomen est omen:* the name is a program, a destiny.

Two episodes help in understanding Jesus' destiny. The first takes place in Capernaum, the city of Jesus, where some people bring a paralytic so that Jesus may heal him (9:1–8). The Master, however, reacts differently than expected, saying to the sick man (in a way bound to cause a stir): "Courage, son, your sins are forgiven." In that man, Jesus seems to glimpse the people as a whole and does not hesitate to put into action that for which he has come. He performs his mission, in full harmony with his name: he saves from sin, the root of every evil.

"But how can a man forgive sin?" object the bystanders. No wonder the scribes said among themselves: "This man is blaspheming!" They did not understand that Jesus could forgive sins because he is Emmanuel, God-with-us.

Jesus Barabbas or Jesus who is called the Christ?

The second episode is connected with the story of the passion, where we encounter another Jesus, "Barabbas" [this name is not included by all authorities or in all translations], who also has a plan of salvation. More than a proper name, Barabbas (*Bar-abbas* in Aramaic) means "son of his father," probably due to a physical or psychological similarity. He is just like his father! Only Matthew calls Barabbas by his proper name, Jesus.[9] And it is meaningful that Barabbas, too, is called Jesus. Both of these men, in fact, want "to save" the people: one from the Romans, the other from their sins. It is the collision of two types of Messiah. "Whom do you want me to release for you," Pilate demands, "Jesus Barabbas or Jesus who is called the Messiah?" (cf. 27:17).

If the first Jesus is "son of his father," whose son is the second? Again, we readers know very well, but Pilate does not and neither does the crowd. And the crowd chooses Jesus Barabbas: a "renowned" prisoner according to Matthew, a "brigand" according to John (18:40). Is this an allusion to the zealots?[10] In any case, which messianism is the rightful one? That of Jesus Barabbas, or of Jesus who is called the Christ?

Pilate washes his hands. And all the people cry out: "His blood be upon us, and upon our children!" (27:25).

---

9. This is a variant that is held as very trustworthy by the Nestle-Aland [Greek New Testament], not noted in the footnote but in the text itself, although between parentheses. See 27:16–17. On the other hand, even Jesus of Nazareth could be called "Barabbas" on the basis of his unique relationship with God the Father, whom Jesus called with affection "Abba" (Mk 14:36). Jesus is Bar-abbà in the theological sense!

10. In Jn 10:2 the same term, "brigand," means whoever enters the sheepfold without passing through the gate, therefore doing violence, not respecting the plan of God. The term could allude to the Zealots, a nationalistic party that wanted liberation from the Romans.

The drama running through the Gospel of Matthew reaches its climax: he who came "to save *his people*" (1:21) faces the rejection of *his people* (*laòs*, the same word).

Nazarene or Nazorean?

A key to this rejection could be the interpretation of the last title given to Jesus the Messiah in the book of his origins: "he shall be called a Nazorean." This is the most common reading, but it is not upheld by any passage of Scripture. It is connected instead to historical tradition. Based on where he came from, Jesus was known as the one from Nazareth, the Nazarene.

This geographical information carries a negative connotation, whether because of the modesty of his family in the eyes of their fellow townspeople, or the modesty of the village itself in the eyes of its neighbors. "When he came to his hometown he taught them in their synagogue, with the result that they were amazed and said, 'Where does this fellow get this wisdom and these mighty works? Is not this the carpenter's son? Is not his mother called Mary, and his brothers James and Joseph and Simon and Judas? And his sisters—are they not all here among us? Where did he get all this?'" (13:54–56).

That the village attracted only modest attention from its contemporaries is obvious in what Nathaniel, an inhabitant of Bethsaida, says to Philip. To the enthusiastic announcement of his friend, "We have found the one Moses wrote about in the Torah, as well as the prophets—Jesus son of

Joseph from Nazareth," Philip objects ironically, "Can anything good come from Nazareth?" (Jn 1:45–46).

"The Nazarene" had to be the title most commonly used to identify Jesus among other men who bore the same name. One can see this in Mark's account of the blind Bartimaeus (10:46–52). There is nothing theological about the information the blind man of Jericho receives from the crowd, only the simple fact of where Jesus was from. And perhaps this explains why Matthew, more inclined to a theological reading of the Scriptures, does not prefer the title "the Nazarene."[11]

"Nazorean," instead, is more in line with Matthew's theological viewpoint.[12] But even this title is not exempt from difficulty, since it finds no reference in any passage from the prophets. Scholars habitually turn to two principal texts: the announcement of the birth of Samson in the Book of Judges, where the title *nazìr* or "consecrated" occurs (Judg 13:5–7), and the messianic oracle of Isaiah, which evokes the compelling image of the *nézer* ("flower, shoot") (11:1).[13]

---

11. Mt 2:23 is the only occurrence—and uncertain at that—in written tradition.

12. M. L. Rigato, "Sarà chiamato Nazoreo (Mt 2:23)," *Ricerche storico bibliche* 4 (1992), 129–141.

13. It is subsequently difficult to be accurate and make a choice between the two possibilities, also because the Greek Scripture never uses the term Nazorean (*nazoràios*), either to translate *nazìr*, or to translate *nézer*. On the other hand, *nazìr* is connected to *nézer*, which is part of the crown placed on the unshaven head of the consecrated person; "their consecration to God is upon their head" (Num 6:7). For this and other semantic and symbolic connections, I refer to *L'identità dei consacrati nella missione della Chiesa e il loro rapporto con il mondo* (Città del Vaticano), 47–66.

Is it a stretch of the imagination to see a convergence of both images in the title "Nazorean"? I don't believe so, at least from the symbolic point of view guiding the "name play" we are dealing with. In Matthew's eyes, Jesus is undoubtedly the *nazîr*, the "consecrated" one par excellence, the *Christos* whom he announces right from the first verses of his Gospel. But Jesus is also the *nézer*, the "shoot" from David's root, the most beautiful "flower" of Nazareth. And so Nazorean and Nazarene both contribute to illustrating the type of Messiah Jesus incarnates. He is the messianic flower-shoot who was born at Bethlehem, the birthplace of David, but who grew up in Nazareth, an unknown village of "Galilee of the Gentiles" (4:15). The two titles express the paradox of Jesus the Messiah, who unites within himself both the royal dignity of "the son of David" and the humility of the "God-with-us" who saves from sin.

Dialoguing with the Word

- Let yourself be drawn into the name play extending from the Gospel account to your own life. What does this son of David, of Abraham, and of Mary mean to you? Who is the Emmanuel for you, the God-with-us and God-with-you?

- Can you say you have encountered the Nazorean in the Nazarene, or rather, the Consecrated of the Lord in the humble figure of the carpenter of Nazareth?

CHAPTER THREE

"In those days"

John and Jesus

(Matthew 3–4)

*T*he last scene in the second chapter of the Gospel of Matthew left us at Nazareth in Galilee, where Joseph found a safe place for Jesus to grow up (2:22–23). But here in chapter 3 a new scene opens in the desert of Judea, where John the Baptist is performing his mission.

Matthew immediately offers an indication of time— "In those days" (3:1).[1] More than to point out a precise chronological moment, this phrase is used to introduce us

---

1. The expression "in those days," as familiar as it is to us, is not in fact very frequent or usual in the Gospel of Matthew. The plural is found only here, while the singular we find in 13:1, where it serves to create a new scene for the section of the parables: "That same day Jesus went out of the house and sat beside the sea"; and in 22:23, where it introduces a new group of adversaries: the Sadducees, who "tempt" Jesus after the Pharisees and the Herodians do so.

to new events (the mission of the Baptist and of Jesus). In fact, there is a leap of almost thirty years (cf. Lk 3:1–2).

The Baptist's encounter with Jesus is described in a kind of triptych also noted in Mark and Luke. The central theme is the rite of baptism (3:13–17), and the two panels on either side of it represent respectively the activity of John in the desert (3:1–12) and the temptation of Jesus in the desert (4:1–11). But our evangelist leaves his signature, so to speak, on this triptych, adding a biblical citation that reveals its theological aspect (4:12–16). This signals a change of scene decisively open to mission: from the desert to the city, from Judea to heathen Galilee.

John, Preacher in the Desert

In those days John the Baptist appeared, preaching in the desert of Judea and saying, "Repent, for the kingdom of heaven is at hand!" He was the one Isaiah the prophet was referring to when he said, "A voice crying out in the desert, 'Prepare the way of the Lord, make straight his paths.'"

John had clothing made from camel hair and wore a leather belt around his waist, and his food was locusts and wild honey. At that time the inhabitants of Jerusalem and all Judea used to go out to him and all the people from the region around the Jordan, and he baptized them in the river Jordan while they confessed their sins.

But when he saw many of the Pharisees and Sadducees coming to be baptized by him he said to them, "You brood of vipers! Who warned you to flee from the coming wrath? Produce evidence of your repentance, then, and do not think you can say to yourselves, 'Abraham is our father,' for I tell you God can raise up children to Abraham from these stones. The ax is already laid to the root of the trees; any tree not producing good fruit will be cut down and thrown into the fire. I baptize you with water as a token of repentance, but the one coming after me is more powerful than I am—I am not worthy to carry his sandals; he will baptize you with the Holy Spirit and fire. His winnowing shovel is in his hand; he will clean out his threshing floor and gather his grain into the barn, but he will burn up the chaff with unquenchable fire" (3:1–12).

Notwithstanding the title immediately associated to his name, John is presented first as a preacher before he is one who baptizes. He is a prophet of the coming Kingdom, as Jesus will be.

Matthew frames these two personalities according to their similarities rather than their differences. Not only does he use the same verb to describe their respective entrance onto the scene (*paraginetai,* "he appears," "he comes": 3:1, 13), the similarity can also be seen with regard to the content of their preaching, summarized by a vigorous call: "Repent, for the kingdom of heaven is at hand." So cries John in the desert (3:2), and with the same words Jesus announces his mission (4:17).

Unlike Mark, who reserves the announcement of the Reign of God to the preaching of Jesus (1:14–15), Matthew is not embarrassed to place this announcement already in the mouth of the Baptist. Both Jesus and John announce "the kingdom of heaven,"[2] calling the people to conver-

---

2. Unlike the other two synoptics, and according to Jewish usage at the time, Matthew prefers the expression "reign of heaven" rather than "reign of God."

sion. They both preach a change of life, a change in the way of acting and above all of thinking: *metanoèite,* "think beyond," "change your mind," "be converted."

The coming of God as savior implies the compelling command: "Convert yourself!"

Regarding the differences between these two personalities, Matthew seems to place them first of all in different contexts or scenes: John appears in the desert (3:1), while Jesus appears (the same verb is used for both) coming from Galilee (3:13). And his mission will begin in Galilee of the Gentiles. (4:17).

So John is strictly connected with the desert. What does such a scene call to mind? In the Old Testament, "the desert" is the place where God educates his people to freedom. It is undoubtedly a dry and impassable place, a demanding training ground, but all the same a salvific space in which YHWH draws up the covenant with Israel. And it is precisely here to the desert that the Baptist, according to the prophetic model in biblical tradition from Hosea to Deutero-Isaiah, again calls the people:

> Therefore, I will now allure her,
> and bring her *into the wilderness,*
> and speak tenderly to her.
> There she shall respond as in the days of her youth,
> as at the time when she came out of the land of Egypt
> —says the LORD—
> you will call me, "My husband,"
> and no longer will you call me, "My Baal"
> (Hos 2:14–16).

Thus says the LORD:
The people who survived the sword
found grace *in the wilderness;*
when Israel sought for rest (Jer 31:2).

A voice cries out:
"*In the wilderness,* prepare the way of the LORD,
make straight in the desert a highway for our God"
(Isa 40:3).

In this setting Matthew places the Baptist, the one who "appears" in the desert because he has the task of preparing the people for their encounter with God. He will outline the conditions for a new covenant that will be ratified by the Messiah with the baptism of fire: the Holy Spirit.

A consistent voice

John is the "voice that cries out," the voice that awakens and stirs souls: *"Prepare the way of the Lord, make his paths straight"* (3:3). This prophet of the desert cries out with everything he has—even his clothing and food: "John had clothing made from camel hair and wore a leather belt around his waist, and his food was locusts and wild honey" (3:4).

John is undoubtedly the embodiment of a basic, fundamental lifestyle, but it is not merely a question of austere poverty. His way of dressing and eating indicates something beyond the ascetical character of his person to a sign of a prophetic duty. In fact, his clothing recalls that of Elijah the prophet (2 Kings 1:8), who in Jewish biblical tradition had the role of preceding the Messiah.

In John, just as in the biblical Elijah, there is an irresistible strength. His voice throws others into crisis, confronts the egoism that allows social injustice, invites conversion, and demands a change in reasoning in order to change behavior and actions. Not by chance are symbols like "way" and "path"—which in the biblical tradition often describe ethical behavior—taken up again.[3] It is precisely the straightening of the *paths* of the mind and the heart that prepare "the way of the Lord."

The prophet of the desert becomes one with the message he announces. He is the voice in perfect harmony with his life, and this unique consistency exercises a powerful force of attraction, inspiring movement, drawing people out of Jerusalem and all of Judea:

> At that time the inhabitants of Jerusalem and all Judea used to go out to him and all the people from the region around the Jordan, and he baptized them in the river Jordan while they confessed their sins. (3:5–6)

A baptism of conversion

A courageous penitential movement is born before it ever becomes baptismal. To whoever comes to him for a *rite*, John in fact speaks in terms of *conversion*.

There is something new here with regard to the traditional Jewish washings that were done through immersion in flowing water. On the banks of the River Jordan there is no place for a rite of self-purification, but for a washing

---

3. Cf. Ex 18:20; Prov 8:13–20; Jer 6:16.

administered by another, who precisely through his "baptizing" comes to be known as the Baptist; this fact already argues against every pretense of self-salvation. Besides, this washing is strictly connected to the confession of sins and the firm will to change one's life: "I baptize you with water as a token of repentance," the Baptist says expressively (3:11).

Mark and Luke attribute the merit of "remission of sins" to the Precursor's baptism (Mk 1:4; Lk 3:3); not so Matthew, for whom Jesus is the only one who can save from sins (1:21). The source of pardon flows from his passion, and it is really his blood that is "poured out for the forgiveness of sins" (26:28: words we read only in Matthew).

John's baptism is meant to prepare the way. Thus it is a rite that demands "fruit worthy of repentance": there is no salvation without personal commitment. These aspects are exemplified in 3:7–10, words addressed to the crowd as in the parallel passage from Luke (3:7–11).[4] But in this instance, two eminent groups of contemporary Judaism are being addressed: "the Pharisees and Sadducees." We are dealing, moreover, with religious movements that are pretty diverse. The first is made up of lay reformers; the second, instead, of functionaries of the Temple, belonging to the Jerusalem aristocracy. Casting his fiery glance in their direction, John addresses them: "Brood of vipers!"—an invective that resounds two other times in the course of the

---

4. After the words addressed to the crowd, Luke reports those addressed to the publicans (3:12–13) and then those addressed to the soldiers (3:14).

Gospel (see 12:34 and 23:33). Men full of mortal venom, how can they escape the divine judgment, "the wrath to come"? What does it matter to brag about having Abraham for a father, a source of blessing for all peoples, if instead of a blessing one is full of venom? The only way to avoid condemnation is a radical change of life, which flourishes in the desert and bears "fruits worthy of repentance" (3:8).

John strips away any false claims of security. God can raise up children to Abraham even from these stones! So there should be no smugness about belonging to an elect people; rather, one should feel the kind of responsibility that demands conversion, because the saving action of God goes beyond every race and culture.[5]

Two images accompany this sharp preaching, which goes straight to personal conscience: the *ax* is already laid to the root of the tree, and the *winnowing fan* is in the hand of the one who is coming. The image of the ax or hatchet needed to cut down the tree suggests that judgment is imminent and therefore conversion cannot be delayed. Jesus will again take up this theme in his first discourse on the mountain: "Every tree not producing good fruit is cut down and thrown into the fire" (7:19).

The second image also refers to the theme of judgment, seen here in the successive stage of the harvest. The

---

5. *To be converted* does not just mean to think good things about the true God, or simply to honor him with words—"Lord, Lord"—but to do what he is waiting for us to do (7:21–23). Matthew does not tire in recalling us to ethical consistency, putting the disciples of the Lord on guard against the dangers of a cultish faith, disconnected from life.

winnowing fan is needed precisely in order to separate the chaff from the grain. The Baptist imagines the one who is coming with this instrument in hand. He envisions an apocalyptic Messiah, whose task it will be to judge humanity, separating the good from the bad as good grain is separated from chaff.[6] In other words, judgment belongs to the one "who comes after [*opìsô*]" and whom John holds to be "more powerful," reprising again the title that is often attributed to God in the Old Testament (cf. Deut 10:17; Neh 1:5).

The Baptist does not exalt himself. His straightforward truth is kneaded with humility. Regarding the Messiah, he does not feel himself worthy even to "carry his sandals." Therefore John does not deceive the large crowd that comes to him to be baptized. His task is to prepare the way, and so his baptism is very different from the Messiah's. And here our evangelist lets us glimpse just how different it is. John baptizes with water for the sake of repentance, but "the one who is more powerful" will baptize with "the Holy Spirit and fire" for the sake of judgment and a new covenant.[7]

---

6. The image of the separation of the good from the bad is also present in the parable of the wise and foolish virgins (25:1–14).

7. For the Baptist, the theme of judgment is strictly connected to the coming of the Messiah. Matthew also supports such a connection, but, in keeping with ancient Christian tradition, he postpones the judgment until the second coming, when the Messiah will return in his glory (25). Therefore, the only criterion for this separation will be the rule of love toward whomever we find in concrete situations of need (25:31–46).

John baptizes Jesus

As already noted, the baptism of Jesus is the central scene of a triptych mentioned by both Mark and Luke, which makes it the debut of the Christ's public activity.

The scene, initially animated and dialogic (3:13–15), develops as a mystery in the second part, outlining the movement in a few essential pictures: Jesus' "coming up" from the water and the "descent" of the Spirit upon him, while from the heavens a voice is heard in the most profound silence saturated with wonder and contemplation (vv. 16–17).

Let us try to immerse ourselves in the passage, in order to envision it more directly and personally, possibly entering on tiptoe so as not to spoil the silence and enchantment of a scene marked by the filial self-awareness of Jesus.

> At that time Jesus came from Galilee to be baptized by John at the Jordan. John tried to prevent him and said, "I need to be baptized by you, and you are coming to me?" But in answer Jesus said to him, "Let it be, for now—it is fitting for us to fulfill all God's will in this way." Then he let him. After he was baptized Jesus at once came up from the water, and, behold, the heavens were opened and he saw the Spirit of God descending upon him like a dove. And behold, a voice from heaven said, "This is my beloved son in whom I am well pleased" (3:13–17).

The dialogue between the Precursor and the Messiah

With the words "at that time" (*tòte*), a phrase characteristic of Matthew's style, he introduces the "appearance" of Jesus who "came from" (*paragìnetai*) Galilee (3:13). He arrives as a stranger in contrast to the Baptist's audience, who come from Jerusalem and Judea (3:5). Jesus arrives from the north, from the region that somewhat disdainfully was called "Galilee of the Gentiles" (4:15), contaminated by pagans. And he comes "to John" with a precise intention: *to be baptized.*

John realizes immediately who is standing in front of him and why, and he tries to avoid the situation. He who comes "after" is "the stronger." Such a reversal of roles inherent in Jesus' request for baptism is unthinkable! This gesture of submission differs greatly from the superiority of the Messiah proclaimed by John, who feels unworthy even to carry his sandals (3:11)!

Only Matthew presents the ensuing dialogue, which allows us to enter into the souls of these two protagonists and dispel all ambiguity. Beneath the dialogue, one can see traces of a problem that later agitated the Christian community: if John's baptism was for conversion, then why did Jesus, who was without sin, ask to be baptized? Our evangelist's answer comes across indirectly in the two men's dialogue and comparison of opinions. On one hand, the Baptist recognizes Jesus' superiority and for this reason "tried to prevent him" from being baptized (indicating repeated attempts to avoid Jesus' request); on the other hand, Jesus persuades John with a mysterious phrase: "It is proper for us in this way to fulfill all righteousness."

These words are remarkable, not only because they are the first pronounced by Jesus in the Gospel of Matthew, but also because they let us glimpse our evangelist's theological viewpoint. Here we see the verb "to fulfill, to accomplish" (*pleròò*), which finds a refrain in the ten citations of fulfillment ("this happened in order to fulfill what was said/written...") and is re-echoed in the Sermon on the Mount, where the Master declares that he has come not to abolish, but to bring to "fulfillment" (5:17). Even the word "justice" or "righteousness" (*dikaiosynê*) takes on a particular importance in Matthew's vocabulary and returns many times in the Sermon on the Mount (cf. 5:6, 10, 20; 6:1, 33). Which justice are we dealing with? Not simply human justice, but something much greater that corresponds to the plan of God. It is the justice revealed in the Gospel, which St. Paul speaks of in his Letter to the Romans (1:17). Matthew, however, also underlines a practical dimension: *justice* expresses a way of acting that conforms to what God considers *just*, and as a consequence implies an attitude of humility and docile obedience that allows God to decide what is appropriate in order to fulfill the mission he is entrusting to us.

It implies an attitude that excludes arrogance and selfish demands. Of the Baptist, Jesus later says: "For John came to you in the way of righteousness [justice]" (21:32). He fulfilled God's will in his mission as precursor, pointing out how to become *just*—but who believed him? *Certainly not you,* says Jesus to the religious leaders and to those who hold positions of power in the Temple of Jerusalem, but "the publicans and prostitutes" did. The same thing happened with Jesus. The great obstacle that interferes with "the way of justice" is not being a sinner but being presumptuous.

Let us return now to the shores of the River Jordan where the Baptist, disconcerted by Jesus' request, hears the answer that, precisely because it overturns roles, will accomplish "all righteousness," or rather the fullness of justice. It is the will of God that Jesus shows his solidarity with sinners who convert themselves to welcome the Kingdom of heaven. And so it is appropriate that the Baptist, as well as his disciples, accept the idea of a meek and humble Messiah, brother of a sinful humanity.[8]

The descent of the Spirit

After this dialogue and Jesus' baptism, heaven intervenes directly to confirm the fullness of justice. Yes, the Father is completely happy with this Son who travels the way of radical solidarity, not disdaining to make himself a brother of sinners, but descending into the water polluted by their sins and purifying them by taking these sins onto himself. *This is precisely the Messiah that I had in mind,* God says in opening the heavens and sending the white dove of the Spirit down upon the head of Jesus.

In reality, Matthew's text is much more elaborated, interwoven with appropriate references to the Scriptures. To the movement of Jesus who "*came up*" from the water corresponds the movement of the Spirit who "*comes down*" from

---

8. Cf. C. Tassin, *Vangelo di Matteo* (Cinisello Balsamo: Edizioni Paoline, 1993), 49.

heaven (that is, from God) and rests upon him (3:16). Why "as a dove"? One's thought rushes spontaneously to the dove sent by Noah over the waters of the flood, which returned with an olive branch in its mouth (Gen 8:11). God wants peace. And Jesus has understood this: "He came and proclaimed the good news of peace to you who were far off, and peace to those who were near" (Eph 2:17).

But what is new to this scene, and what scholars debate over, is the symbolic connection of the Spirit-dove, absent in the account of the deluge. Where did this connection originate? The idea takes us back even further, to the first verses of Genesis, where it is said that "the Spirit of God was hovering over the waters." Here, however, it is the act of hovering that reminds us of the Spirit, and not the form he took, which remains vague. We are not told what the Spirit of God resembles as he hovers over the water.

In reality it wasn't in the Bible that the image of the dove was put in direct relationship with the Spirit, but in the Judaic texts. One reads in the Babylonian Talmud: "And the Spirit of God hovered over the surface of the waters as a dove hovers over her young without touching them" (Hag 15a). From here the step is a short one: the dove becomes the symbol of the Spirit that comes to rest on the Messiah.[9]

In his book of the origins of the Messiah, Matthew already introduced us to this kind of up-to-date reading of the Bible. We already know that Jesus was "conceived by the Holy Spirit" (1:18–20), but the new scene seems to be

---

9. So also in the *Odi di Salomone* (24:1–2), a Judeo-Christian writing from the end of the first century after Christ.

an investiture. The Spirit himself comes down from heaven and rests on Jesus: "The spirit of the Lord shall rest on him," Isaiah wrote in reference to Emmanuel, "the spirit of wisdom and understanding, the spirit of counsel and might, the spirit of knowledge and the fear of the Lord" (11:2). Our evangelist, who already spoke of Emmanuel, seems now to also point out the fulfillment of this prophetic page: the Spirit comes to rest *upon him.*

Some commentators identify the setting of the baptismal scene in that re-reading of the Exodus in Isaiah, where we find the agonizing cry: "O that you would tear open the heavens and come down" (64:1). We also find here the only passage in the Old Testament according to which the Spirit of the Lord "comes down" upon the people and "leads" them into the desert (63:14). "Baptized and then 'led' by the Spirit into the desert, Jesus seemed to be the leader of a fresh exodus of those who would follow him along the road to a new *justice.*"[10]

One thing does not exclude the other. Indeed, these and other events can be envisioned as a sequence of dissolving scenes.

The voice of the Father

After the vision ("and he saw," 3:16) there follows a voice, and then everything is wrapped in silence. Without a doubt we are at the high point of this story, and the divine voice offers the decisive key to interpret it.

---

10. Tassin, *Vangelo di Matteo,* 50.

It should be noted that this is the first time where the testimony to Jesus' identity is not backed up with a biblical citation, but by the *living voice* of God. But to whom is this testimony directed? Not to Jesus himself, as it is in the parallel versions of Mark and Luke: "You are my beloved Son, in you I am well pleased." The voice in Matthew does not say "you are" but "this is." The voice addresses a third person, who could be the Baptist but could also be the Gospel audience. It is to us that the Father addresses his testimony to Jesus' identity.

To profoundly understand the meaning of what this voice is saying, the reader must allow him or herself to be led again to the pages of Scripture where the unique voice of the Father resounds.

Three texts offer a background to this scene. First, Psalm 2, which describes the statutes of sonship for the Messiah: "You are my son; today I have begotten you" (v. 7). This particular relationship with God is fundamental to the Messiah's salvific mission. One thus understands the importance of this testimony at the beginning of Jesus' ministry. At different times in the course of the Gospel he is declared or is recognized as "son,"[11] but only here, and later at the transfiguration (17:5), is this identity confirmed by the divine voice.

---

11. Jesus declares himself "Son" in 11:27; 24:36; 28:19. He is recognized (or provoked to show himself) as "Son of God" by the tempter (4:3, 6), by the possessed (8:29), by the disciples (14:33), by Peter (16:16), by the High Priest (26:63), by passersby as he carries the cross (27:40, 43), and finally by the centurion (27:54).

The voice adds something that is missing from the psalm: Jesus is not only the "son," but a son who is "beloved, favored" (*agapêtòs*). The same expression is used for the long-awaited son whom God asked of Abraham in sacrifice: "Take your son, your only son...whom you love...and offer him as a burnt offering..." (Gen 22:2). Jesus is the only Son, the beloved, of whom Isaac is a figure. Isaac allows us to see where Jesus' love will take him.

Finally, Jesus is declared the joy and satisfaction of the Father, "the one in whom I am well pleased." And here the heavenly voice borrows again from the prophet Isaiah the beginning of the first song of the Servant of the Lord:

Here is my servant, whom I uphold,
my chosen, in whom my soul delights;
I have put my spirit upon him;
he will bring forth justice to the nations (Isa 42:1).

All of this is a sophisticated weaving of biblical citations that goes from a hermeneutical setting to the voice from the heavens, in itself is already a wonderful synthesis, because it also works in the theme of the Spirit. On this chosen servant, in whom the Lord is pleased, the Spirit of the Lord rests and works for the sake of a universal mission that concerns not only Israel, but also "the nations."

Dialoguing with the Word

- Place yourself spiritually on the banks of the River Jordan in order to deepen in prayer the scene of Jesus' baptism. Listen again with calm to the

dialogue between John and Jesus, between the
Precursor and the Messiah.

- Contemplate that dove of peace that comes to rest
on Jesus' head. He is the visible sign of the Father's
pleasure in the new humanity rising out of the water.
The Spirit of the Lord also rests upon you. Are you
aware of his presence? How do you live this relation
ship with the Holy Spirit, who has been communi-
cated to you by Christ through the sacraments of
Baptism and Confirmation?

Jesus defeats the tempter

From the shores of the Jordan Jesus departs alone, just
as he had arrived alone. There are no witnesses to his
lenten experience in the desert, an experience that profoundly marked his life, as he himself would later tell his
disciples. It is a time of intimacy with God, his Father, in
complete dependence on him who gives everything, overcoming all trials and temptations the desert holds in store.

We are at the last scene in the triptych that introduces
the mission of Jesus. This scene is connected to the preceding one by a double verse explaining that it is the Spirit
who leads Jesus toward the place of trial, and that the so-
called "temptations" deal expressly with his being "the Son
of God." Therefore, what comes into play is the verification of what we have just heard and contemplated in the
scene of the baptism.

Then Jesus was led into the desert by the Spirit to be
tempted by the devil. After fasting for forty days and forty

nights he at last became hungry, and the tempter approached him and said, "If you are the Son of God, tell these stones to become loaves of bread." But in answer Jesus said, "It is written, *Not by bread alone shall man live, but by every utterance proceeding from the mouth of God.*" Then the devil took him to the holy city. He set him on the parapet of the Temple and said to him, "If you are the Son of God, throw yourself down, for it is written, *He will give his angels orders concerning you, and on their hands they will carry you, lest you strike your foot against a stone.*" Jesus said to him, "It is further written, *You shall not tempt the Lord your God!*" So then the devil took him up a very high mountain and showed him all the kingdoms of the world and their splendor, and he said to him, "All theses things I will give you, if you will fall down and worship me!" But Jesus said to him, "Be gone, Satan! For it is written, *The Lord your God shall you worship, and him alone shall you adore.*" Then the devil left him and, behold, angels came and served him (4:1–11).

Matthew highlights an uncomfortable fact: the Spirit leads Jesus into the desert precisely "to be tempted by the devil." Mark limits himself to saying that the Spirit "drove him out into the desert" (Mk 1:12). Luke also is more mellow, although in agreement in what the background indicates: "Jesus returned from the Jordan full of the Holy Spirit and was led by the Spirit through the desert for forty days, while being tempted by the devil" (Lk 4:1–2). So Matthew's account immediately provokes the question: Why does the Spirit of God lead this beloved Son into the tempter's camp, into the arms of Satan? Shouldn't the Spirit of God (at least we'd like to think so) protect and defend him? Why instead does the Spirit lead the newly baptized to meet with the devil, who divides and confuses the order desired by the Creator, as the Greek name *diàbolos* suggests?

"My child, when you come to serve the Lord, prepare yourself for testing," admonishes that great wise man of the Bible, Jesus ben Sirach (Sir 2:1). Temptations come in order "to prove" if the decision to serve God and one's brothers and sisters is truly consistent.

The desert's compelling scene

We are not told the specific geographical aspects of the desert into which Jesus is led under the guidance of the Spirit. This absence of information helps to create a setting against which Matthew weaves a subtle parallel, contrasting Israel's behavior with that of Jesus.

In fact, the desert, it is remembered, is the place where the community of Israel was formed after the crossing of the sea and the "tests" that accompanied their journey.[12] It is a place for training and also a place of trials, a testing of the choices of faith, because the one who is "tempted/tried" is obviously exposed to the possibility of sinning, of giving in, of not holding up under the test. Thus it was for the people of Israel during the forty years of pilgrimage in the desert, so much so that God complained about them in these terms:

> For forty years I loathed that generation
> and said, "They are a people whose hearts go astray,

---

12. See in particular Ex 15:22; 17:7, with the complaint about the water and the food, and 32, with the rebellion and the golden calf; similarly, Num 11 and 20:1–13.

and they do not regard my ways."
Therefore in my anger I swore,
"They shall not enter my rest" (Ps 95:10–11).

The place of divine rest symbolizes the Promised Land, into which none of those who had come out of Egypt, not even Moses, could enter. "The Spirit of the Lord" who was present at the crossing of the sea "guided them to their rest" (Isa 63:14), but through trials or temptations in the desert. And the chosen people did not overcome these trials. Jesus instead does not disappoint the Spirit who has come to rest on him and who has led him into the desert. He overcomes the temptations and defeats the tempter, completely confirming the filial identity revealed at his baptism.

Having now established the outline of the reading, we are better equipped to appreciate the individual elements of this scene, beginning with the "fast."

Fasting and a hunger for God

In the great religious traditions, both biblical and non-biblical, fasting has nothing in common with our modern culture of dieting. Rather, it exists to underscore one's total dependence on God, who gives both life and nourishment. Therefore, the lent of Jesus (like every lent that is truly observed!) first of all involves the way of fasting. He who will be accused by his enemies of being a "glutton and a drunkard" (11:19) in reality knows through direct experience and conscious choice the pangs of hunger: "He ate nothing during those days, and when they were completed he was hungry" (4:2).

Forty is the biblical number of trial and fasting.[13] But the words of Matthew (the only evangelist to explicitly say "forty days and forty nights") allow us to glimpse the symbolic connection to the compelling figure of Moses, who before receiving the divine revelation on the mountain "was there with the LORD forty days and forty nights; he neither ate bread nor drank water" (Ex 34:28; Deut 9:9). Jesus, who will teach from the mountain with an authority superior to that of Moses, prepares for his mission in the same way: with fasting and prayer.

The words *desert* and *fasting* evoke each other; the desert with its dryness expresses the great fast of a ground deprived of its vital element. In this setting the awareness of complete dependence on the one who gives water, life, and nourishment is inevitable. And to experience in one's own stomach the acute pangs of hunger helps one to better feel another and more primordial hunger: that for God and for his word.

In Matthew's account, the tempter approaches Jesus after his long fast of *forty days and forty nights,* not before. It's as if Matthew is saying that if Jesus unmasked deceit and defeated it, perhaps it is because he also knows how to persevere in fasting and in prayer. Later, the Master will in fact teach his disciples that there are some kinds of demons that cannot be defeated except "with prayer and fasting" (17:21).

---

13. Apart from what is in the Bible, Judaic texts also verify this, as in the *Apocolypse of Abraham* 12:1 and the *Testament of Isaac* 4:4.

A duel using Scripture

Unlike Mark, who does not specify the number or nature of the temptations, Matthew and Luke agree that there are three of them. And the first arrives precisely when Jesus feels hungry: "If you are the Son of God, tell these stones to become loaves of bread." With satanic irony, stretching his gaze along the dry expanse of rocks that form the desert of Judah, the tempter proposes the transformation of stones into bread; there would be enough to last forever! But the root of the temptation is more subtle. Jesus is challenged to validate himself by demonstrating the power inherent in his divine origins. *If you are the one the divine voice said you are, then exercise your power.*

At different times in the course of his mission, Jesus will be tempted this way—not only by enemies who challenge him beneath the cross to prove his Messianic power ("Save yourself! If you are the Son of God, come down from the cross!": 27:40), but also by his friends. The very same Peter, who, after having proclaimed him Messiah and Son of God discourages him from following the way of the cross, merits the name of "satan" (16:22–23).

Jesus' answer to the first temptation is an anticipation of victory over the various attacks that come to him from this utilitarian way of thinking. Jesus calls on the Word of God, in this case Deuteronomy 8:3, a verse that is part of a splendid meditation on the meaning of the hunger Israel suffered in the desert. It is helpful to read the passage in its context:

> Remember the long way that the LORD your God has led
> you these forty years in the wilderness, in order to humble
> you, testing you to know what was in your heart, whether or
> not you would keep his commandments. He humbled you
> by letting you hunger, then by feeding you with manna,
> with which neither you nor your ancestors were acquainted,
> in order to make you understand that one does not live by
> bread alone, but by every word that comes from the mouth
> of the LORD (Deut 8:2–3).

There is no misunderstanding here. It is not a matter of belittling the value of bread but of affirming the primacy of the creative Word, of a God who wants the good of his people and who takes care of them, as the miracle of the manna proves. And Jesus, contrary to the people who gave in to the temptation of hunger (cf. Ex 16, the episode of manna), confirms his full adherence to the Word of God, placing total trust in the Father.

But the devil doesn't give up; "to tempt" is his trade, and he knows how to do it well. His ability to touch the most sensitive chord of the human psyche is remarkable. There is always something surprising and fascinating in what we call "temptations," as in the forbidden fruit that was beautiful to look at and good to eat (Gen 3:6).

And so the devil makes another attempt with a kind of flight to Jerusalem, to the pinnacle of the Temple, where one can enjoy the best view of the holy city and can move around the sanctuary, the so-called religious world. The tempter, to whom this world is well known, suggests a spectacular act that will bring Jesus immediate recognition of his messianic identity: "Throw yourself down!" This time the devil also cites Scripture; he has learned the trade. The passage he cites guarantees divine protection to the faithful one who trusts in the Lord, and also challenges what Jesus has just declared. *Do you really trust in the Lord? Then no harm will come to you if you throw yourself down, because God will send his angels.*

> No evil shall befall you,
> no scourge come near your tent.
> For he will command his angels concerning you
> to guard you in all your ways.
> On their hands they will bear you up,
> so that you will not dash your foot against a stone
> (Ps 91:10–12).

There is nothing to add; the citation is precise. But this temptation contains a flaw: the exploitation of the Word of God, something which, sad to say, religious men and women have often been guilty of in the course of history. Jesus unmasks Satan, who pretends to be an expert on the Scriptures, by using the same weapon—another citation of Moses: "Do not put the LORD your God to the test" (Deut 6:16). God is not to be tempted; he is not to be put to the test by challenging him or expecting miracles from him. Instead, he is to be obeyed.

And so we come to the third temptation, situated on "a very high mountain." Here the devil, seeing himself humiliated in the holy city, does not use the armor of Scripture but directly exposes himself. He speaks as a great master, promising the whole world and its glory—precisely what Psalm 2:6–8 attributes to the Messiah: the possession of all the kingdoms of the earth. He only stipulates one condition: that Jesus fall down and worship him! At this point Jesus, having been patient until now, explodes in a vehement "Away with you, Satan!" And he throws in the devil's face the reason for his refusal, drawing from Scripture one more time: "For it is written, 'The LORD your God shall you worship, and him alone shall you adore'" (cf. Deut 6:13).[14]

The conclusion of the story sees the devil departing and angels drawing near, who "came and served him." The verb in the original language, *diakonéô*, suggests a *special service to God* (1 Tm 3:10) rather than a *table service* (Acts 6:2). Concretely, Jesus' hunger is answered by heaven, just as the people in the desert were nourished by manna, the "bread of angels."

The account of the temptations ends therefore on an unidentified *mountain,* with angels serving Jesus. Matthew will also conclude the Gospel on a *mountain,* with the Risen One surrounded not by angels but by his disciples, to whom he reveals that he has "all power in heaven and on earth" (28:18)—even power over death, which is a good deal more than the devil had promised him.

---

14. Significantly, three times Jesus alludes to Moses, all references to Deuteronomy, in biblical tradition is considered the spiritual testament of the great leader of the Exodus. Matthew keeps to the comparison of Jesus with Moses, already put forward in the infancy accounts (searched for on the part of Herod, who wanted to kill him, just as Pharaoh wanted to kill Moses). Perhaps the choice of a mountain as the place of the third temptation (unlike Luke, who places it in Jerusalem) could suggest an allusion to Mount Nebo, from the top of which Moses saw the Promised Land and died without being able to enter it, having also given in to temptation (Deut 34). Jesus, instead, overcoming every trial, is able to lead all those who follow him in his exodus into the final Promised Land.

Jesus does not use his power to subjugate others, as Satan suggested he should do and as the "great ones" of other nations do ("You know that the rulers of the Gentiles lord it over them, and their leaders exercise authority over them": 20:25). Instead, Jesus sends his disciples to all peoples, so that everyone may share in the life of love flowing from the Holy Trinity.

Dialoguing with the Word

- Jesus overcame the devil's temptations in full obedience to the Father and his word. And you? Reflect on how you behave when faced with temptations.

- Renew your baptismal promises with which you can express your commitment to renounce Satan, his tricks and vanities.

In Galilee of the Gentiles

The news of the Baptist's imprisonment by Herod Antipas makes the hour strike for Jesus' mission. From Judea "he withdraws" (*anechòresen*) to Galilee and begins his preaching. Now that John has been silenced, the announcement of the Reign of God and the consequent call for conversion resounds in the mouth of Jesus: "Repent [*metanoéite*], for the kingdom of heaven is at hand" (4:17).

They are the same words the Baptist used (3:2), but the scene is different. The call to conversion reverberates now in the city rather than in the desert. Jesus, in fact, begins his mission by leaving the outlying village of Nazareth and

going to live in Capernaum, more centrally located on the
northeast edge of the Sea of Galilee.

> When Jesus heard that John had been arrested he returned to
> Galilee. He left Nazareth and went and settled in Caper-
> naum by the sea, in the regions of Zebulon and Naphtali, to
> fulfill what was said by Isaiah the prophet, when he said,
> *Land of Zebulon and land of Naphtali, the sea road, beyond the
> Jordan, Galilee of the Gentiles, the people living in darkness have
> seen a great light, and for those living in the land and shadow of
> death a light has dawned upon them.* From that time on Jesus
> began to preach and to say, "Repent, for the kingdom of
> heaven is at hand!" (4:12–17)

A decisive transfer

The Messiah of Israel begins his preaching in Galilee—
not in Nazareth, where he was known as the son of the carpenter, but in Capernaum. "Near the sea," writes Matthew,
who on one hand uses the Hebraic way of calling the lake
"the sea" and, on the other, re-echoes the prophecy of Isaiah
8:23, which mentions the "road to the sea." Actually, in
Capernaum a milestone was found that belonged to a fork
in the *Via Maris,* the great highway of communication
between Egypt and Mesopotamia. From the coast it rose
up to the region of the Lake of Tiberius, making it one of
the most trafficked areas of Galilee, open to commercial
and cultural exchanges.

Matthew gives great importance to Jesus moving to
Capernaum. It is a strategic decision for his mission, but
above all it is done to accomplish the plan of God (v. 14).
The prophet Isaiah announced an optimistic reversal in

situation for the territory of Zebulun and Naphtali, precisely where we find Capernaum, chosen by Jesus as the center of his activity. In this territory, a place of violence and death at the time of the Assyrian deportation,[15] a light will shine.

In the prophet's vision, images are superimposed one on another. The night of banishment is a reminder, by way of contrast, of the night of liberation, that is, the luminous night of Gideon and his troops, when three hundred men with lighted lanterns let out an immense shout (cf. Judg 7:20)! This was enough to put the enemy to flight "as on the day of Midian" (Isa 9:4). And so it will be again, since the prophet announces the birth of a baby who carries the sign of royalty (a descendent of King David) and who is called "the mighty God and prince of peace" (Isa 9:5).[16]

In the evangelist's rereading of the text, the hope nourished by the prophet takes a leap forward. If for Isaiah the phrase "the people who walked in darkness" evokes the tragic situation of the exiles, Matthew sees it as a metaphor describing a condition of ignorance and separation from God. But the connection is still valid: there, where darkness reigned, a light is shining.

---

15. The text of Isa 8:23—9:1 seems to allude to the military campaign of Tiglat Pilezer, which culminated in the Assyrian deportation in 732 B.C. (cf. 2 Kings 15:29).

16. In the first two chapters of the Gospel of Matthew, Jesus is already presented as the "God-with-us" (1:23); now he is seen to fulfill the text of Isaiah, which announced the kind of activity/work to be carried out by Emmanuel, the "God-with-us."

Matthew is drawn to the theme of light, which for him means the brightness of fulfillment. A star guides the Magi to Bethlehem, to the newborn shepherd-king, and when Jesus begins his preaching the light shines on a people who lie in the shadows. A cry of joy runs through Galilee of the Gentiles; it is the joyful announcement of the Gospel. And immediately there is light.

The call of the first disciples

The first thing Jesus does is call four men to follow him, to share his mission and his destiny. Matthew sees a strict connection between the call of the first disciples and the announcement of the Reign that demands conversion. This is a narrative connection, because the account is introduced right afterward, but it is also more profound than that. The fact that these men immediately leave everything to follow the one who calls them proves that they are ready to radically change their way of thinking and, like Jesus, stake their destiny on the coming Reign of heaven.[17]

Matthew's account runs parallel to Mark's and is told in two scenes, both of which take place along the sea in Capernaum. Jesus is walking, with his gaze open to the

---

17. It is the same in Mark, where the call of the first disciples (1:16–20) follows the announcement of the coming reign of God (1:14–15). The tradition handed down by the first two evangelists does not see Jesus without disciples. Not so in Luke, according to whom at the beginning Jesus works alone: he preaches in the synagogue of Nazareth (4:14–30), performs miracles at Capernaum (4:31–44), and calls the first disciples only after the miraculous catch of fish (5:1–11).

world around him and to the fishermen intent on casting their nets into the sea or hauling them to shore. He passes alongside daily life molded by work and fatigue, but also by hope, and encounters people. He passes as God knows how to pass, with a penetrating and creative gaze.

Christianity really begins this way, with Jesus who passes by, sees, and calls others to follow him. It begins with four fishermen of Galilee, two sets of brothers ready to leave their world and everything it represents: work, family, social position, financial security, affective stability.... It begins with *leaving all* in order to follow, unconditionally, this young rabbi from Nazareth who could not have fully understood their trade—he was a carpenter!—yet who promises just the same to make them "fishers of men."

> Now as he was walking along the Sea of Galilee he saw two brothers—Simon, who is called Peter, and his brother Andrew—casting a throw net into the sea—they were fishermen. And he said to them, "Follow me, and I will make you fishers of men." So they left their nets at once and followed him. He continued on from there and saw two more brothers, James son of Zebedee and his brother John, mending their nets in the boat with their father Zebedee, and he called them. They left the boat and their father at once and followed him (4:18–22).

Jesus passes by and sees the person before he ever sees what he or she does; this is why a person's proper name contains something unique and unrepeatable. He sees Simon and Andrew, and then James and John. He sees and calls them by name as the Creator does the stars (Ps 146:4; Bar 3:35) and as the Good Shepherd calls his sheep (Jn 10:3). This way of seeing is equivalent to a loving knowledge based on the solid trust that the Master places in those he calls to follow him.

It is beautiful to note that the first "vocations" were two sets of brothers. The call of Jesus goes out in plural. He sees in the singular (i.e., Simon, Andrew) and calls to community. The Christian vocation, in fact, is a call to a broad fraternity, with a mission to search for others. The Master calls others to follow him in order to become "fishers of men." I imagine he gave this phrase the flavor of a challenge, smiling while he continued to walk with his disciples along the lake in the morning breeze. What does he mean "to fish" for people, and how is it done? Jesus doesn't slow down to explain. They will find out by following him, day after day.

The response of those who were first called is an exemplary one for disciples of every age. Promptly (*euthèòs*, "immediately") they left everything: nets, boat, neighbors, and even father, who in society at that time represented the supreme point of reference and of family unity. At a word they left not only their trade but also the social identity closely connected to it (for the people of Capernaum, Simon was "the fisherman") and their family ties. For these first disciples, to follow the Master meant a response signaling the end of one way of life and the beginning of another. Everything suddenly became relative to their call. Even the most precious things would be put aside for the sake of entrusting oneself with unlimited faith to the God who was encountered in the Gospel preached by Jesus.

> ## *Dialoguing with the Word*
>
> - Place yourself on the shore of the Sea of Galilee and allow yourself to be surprised by Jesus who is passing by. He sees you as you are, with your personal history and relationships, in your family and social situation, with the fatigues and hopes that make up your day. Let his gaze reach your heart. Listen to the sound of your name, as only he can pronounce it, with that creative love that still—and always—calls to life. Jesus calls you to make an "exodus," to leave not for the sake of leaving, but in order to follow him.

Announcing the Good News

He traveled throughout Galilee, teaching in their synagogues, proclaiming the good news of the kingdom, and healing every disease and illness among the people. News of him went out through all Syria, and they brought him all who were sick with various diseases and were suffering torments—the demon-possessed, epileptics, paralytics—and he healed them (4:23–24).

Here we see an overview of Jesus' activities in Galilee and of the enthusiastic welcome he received from the crowds! Jesus is described as an itinerant preacher going through all of Galilee. To what purpose? Three kinds of verbs are specified: "teaching, preaching, healing" (*didáskôn, kêryssôn, therapèuôn*), a sequence that returns identically in 9:35.[18]

---

18. Mt 4:23 and 9:35 are two summary parallels that respectively open and close the Sermon on the Mount (5–7) and the series of ten miracles (8–9), in which the evangelist illustrates that the teaching and healings are two complimentary aspects of Jesus' mission.

For Matthew the figure of the Master is definitely in the foreground, obvious by two out of the three verbs mentioned. But it is surprising that teaching precedes announcement. Don't we usually say the exact opposite, that first comes the *kerygma* and then the *didachê;* first the announcement and then the catechesis or teaching? This unusual order leads us to assume that the evangelist wants *announcement* to be the soul of Jesus' whole pastoral action, and not a first priority that is replaced by a second. In the order of sequence, in fact, *kêryssôn* occupies the central place, meaning that at the center of the entire mission—teaching and healing—is the announcement of the good news that God comes to save his people.

The teaching takes place in the synagogue. The complex language Matthew uses, typical of a summary, does not name a specific synagogue, as does Mark who specifies Capernaum (Mk 1:21) and Luke who mentions Nazareth (Lk 4:16). Matthew, instead, notes the Master's presence in different synagogues spread out over the villages of Galilee.[19] Obviously Jesus teaches out in the open also, on a hilltop or on the seashore, but the synagogue is the place where the Judaic community habitually gathers on the Sabbath, and still gathers today, to listen to the Word of God. Unlike the liturgy of the Temple, which is based on sacrifice, that of the synagogue is centered on the Word.

19. See the synthesis of P. Kaswalder, "La Sinagoga di Cafarnao" (Mk 1:21–39) and the archaeological problem of the "Galilean synagogue," in *Entrarono a Cafarnao: Lettura interdisciplinare di Mc 1. Studi in onore di P. Virginio Ravanelli,* edited by M. Adinolfi and P. Kaswalder (Jerusalem: Franciscan Printing Press, 1997), 243–271.

But why does Matthew specify "in *their* synagogue"? The phrase seems to suggest a conflict of interests or a situation of opposition (yours, not ours!) that doesn't reflect the time of Jesus, but existed instead at the time of the evangelist.[20] In point of fact, Jesus often went to the synagogue of Nazareth, where he had been raised (cf. Lk 4:16–30), and afterward to the synagogue of Capernaum, mere steps from Peter's house. This phrase, therefore, seems related to the time during which the Gospel was written.

Two historical levels—the time of Jesus and of the Church—merge together in the narration. Matthew passes from one to the other without warning, but some signs, such as the one above, inform the attentive reader that a certain tension had arisen. What had happened in the meantime?

In A.D. 70 a catastrophe took place: the Temple of Jerusalem was destroyed, throwing into crisis the religious institutions attached to it. Judaism was obliged to rethink itself from an entirely new basis. From this phase of critical rethinking emerged a religiosity of the pharisaical kind, which was connected to the school or academy that had its seat in Jamnia, on the Mediterranean coast. In the context of this revision, certain disciplinary measures were taken against the followers of the *Nazarene,* in particular a kind

---

20. The contrast is explicit in the discourse against the scribes and Pharisees, where the designation "in their synagogues" (23:34) is connected to the experience of persecution. It can also be seen in 7:29, where it speaks of "their scribes," and 22:7, where Jerusalem is designated as "their city."

of excommunication that excluded them from the synagogue, branding them as heretics and slanderers. The fourth Gospel alludes to such a situation in the account of the man born blind. In fact, his parents' diplomatic response ("Ask him, he's old enough to speak for himself") is explained by the evangelist in the following way: "His parents said these things because they were afraid of the Jews, for the Jews had already agreed that anyone who declared Jesus to be the Messiah would be banished from the synagogue" (Jn 9:22).

Some additions in the Judaic prayer called the *Shmoné esrè*—the "Eighteen blessings"—seem to be from this period, in particular the twelfth regarding "the Nazarenes and the heretics," which sounds decidedly like a curse:

> May there be no hope for apostates; eradicate promptly from our days the reign of pride; and may the Nazarenes and the heretics perish in an instant. May they be cancelled from the book of the living and with the just not be written. Blessed are you, YHWH, who humble the proud![21]

Let us return to our evangelist, for whom it is more important to explain *why* than *where*. Jesus teaches, "preaching and curing the sick." He is at the same time teacher and healer, doctor and compassionate shepherd. This Jesus who welcomes and cures the sick recalls the figure of the Servant of the Lord who takes upon himself the infirmities of his people, as the citation from Isaiah 53:4,

---

21. R. Penna, *L'ambiente storico-culturale delle origini cristiane* (Bologna: EDB, 2000), 31.

which is placed at the end of the first series of healings, explicitly points out (8:17). Christ's pastoral charity—his great kindness and mercy—is proof of his teaching. What he teaches, he himself does—or rather, he *is*: love that cares for, that listens to and comforts.

This is how the Good News traveled swiftly throughout all of Galilee and the Jordan, reaching the territory of the Decapolis and even Syria (4:24–25). And in response to this, crowds gathered—people hungry for the truth and marked with sorrow. A great success, yes, but how did Jesus react? How did he behave after such success? *Where* does he lead the crowd, *how* does he guide them? The next scene, which introduces the Sermon on the Mount, answers this question.

Dialoguing with the Word

- The beginnings of Jesus' mission in Galilee are marked by an openness to people. The Lord's openness is obvious in his great ability to welcome others. People very different from one another come to him. As Jesus does, so too the Church is called to reach out to all peoples...

CHAPTER FOUR

"Blessed are the poor"

Jesus dreams of his community

(Matthew 5–7)

*T*he beginning of Jesus' preaching in Galilee was accompanied by great success, so much so that his fame spread as far as Syria, Matthew notes. But how did Jesus respond to this success? Where was he leading the multitudes that followed him?

He went up the mountain

"When [Jesus] saw the crowds he went up the mountain" (5:1). This is the first time the Master decides to go up the mountain. Actually, we saw him on the mountain in the preceding chapter, in the scene of the fourth temptation. But in that instance Jesus did not have a choice; he was taken there by another: "The devil took him up a very high mountain" (4:8). Now, instead, he leads others to the mountain of the Beatitudes.

The scene is strongly evocative. As Moses went up Mount Sinai to receive the divine revelation, the *Torah,* so the new Moses *goes up* the mountain. Whoever wants to follow him must also go up. Jesus has to go up to a higher place, even if, next to the majesty of Sinai, which rises almost seven thousand feet, a mountain of Galilee like the one identified as the Mount of the Beatitudes was much lower. Obviously we are dealing here more with a symbolic sense than with something quantifiable—a going up whereby Jesus' words trace a strong *ethic* to carry out a greater justice. It is also a "going up" with greater hope, full of expectation for the Kingdom that is coming. Therefore, let us climb after Jesus, Master and Shepherd of life, along with multitudes of every age.

"After he sat down his disciples came to him" (5:1b). The second scene of this solemn debut describes Jesus as seated (*kathìsantos*) at the top of the hill, with his disciples around him. Using the verb *kathìzô* (from which the word "cathedra" stems), the evangelist already lets us know that Jesus did not sit down to rest but to teach. He is the Teacher around whom the disciples press; they seem to hang on his every word. In fact, Matthew continues in a solemn manner: "And he opened his mouth [*to stòma*] and taught them [*edìdasken*], saying..." (5:2).

This image was the inspiration for the magnificent mosaic decorating the apse of St. Apollinaris Church in Rome. In the mosaic, the disciples are depicted as sheep that the Master feeds with his word. But to whom is Jesus speaking? Who benefits from this *Sermon on the Mount?*[1] Is it meant only for the disciples, or also for the crowds?

Here, however, the text does not mention the crowds. Where are they? Did they stay behind in the valley, or have they also gone up the mountain? Matthew does not mention them until the end of the entire discourse, when the crowd again appears on the scene to express wonder and amazement: "And it happened that when Jesus had finished these words the crowds were amazed at his teaching because he was teaching them on his own authority, and not like their scribes" (7:28–29). This then indicates that they were present and were listening all along.

So, narratively speaking, the crowds were present although in the background with regard to the disciples. It will be up to the disciples to act as a bridge between Jesus and the crowds, so that they no longer limit themselves to expressing amazement and satisfaction at the Master's teaching, but will also be drawn to loving faith, moving from admirers to disciples personally committed to following him.

In messianic times, the Jews expected a pilgrimage of people to the mountain of the Lord with the precise intention of learning the Law, or rather, of learning to live in a way pleasing to the Lord.

---

1. G. Lohfink, *Per chi vale il Discorso della Montagna?* (Brescia: Queriniana, 1990). See also G. Giavini, *Ma io vi dico: Esegesi e vita attorno al Discorso della Monatagna* (Milan: Editrice Ancora, 1993).

Many peoples shall come and say,
"Come, let us go up to the mountain of the Lord,
to the house of the God of Jacob;
that he may teach us his ways
and that we may walk in his paths" (Isa 2:3; and a similar
text in Mi 4:2).

One catches a glimpse of this prophecy from Isaiah in the precise scenery Matthew uses to introduce the Master's first discourse, even if the mountain is not the Temple but a hill of Galilee. A great crowd of diverse ethnic extraction (not only from Judea, but also from Syria and the Decapolis: 4:23–25) goes up the mountain behind Jesus to learn how to live in a way pleasing to the Lord.

The Beatitudes: subversive joy

Jesus' first words on the mountain are a cry of joy: *makàrioi*, "blessed"! Who are blessed? Who are those whom Jesus proclaims happy? People whom we would never hesitate to judge unfortunate: the poor, the afflicted, the suffering, the hungry—as many who followed him must have been, given the summary immediately preceding: "and they brought him all who were sick with various diseases and were suffering torments—the demon-possessed, epileptics, paralytics..." (Mt 4:24).

Before this crowd, Jesus breaks into a cry of joy. Here Matthew succeeds in linking two contrasting images: the solemnity of the scene, which suits the authority of the Master, and a face that is bursting with joy, because one can't say "blessed, happy!" with a serious, much less a sad, face. Therefore, this Master is serious about what he says, but extremely joyous with regard to *how* he says and lives it. The beloved Son of the Father is joyful. He understands the "game" God is playing on behalf of his poor and afflicted ones—a "game" he will ultimately win. Therefore Jesus sings the Beatitudes. He inaugurates a new way of seeing life from a viewpoint of hope that does not disappoint.

> "Blessed are the poor in spirit, for theirs is the kingdom of heaven.
> Blessed are those who mourn, for they shall be comforted.
> Blessed are the meek, for they shall inherit the earth.
> Blessed are those who hunger and thirst to do God's will, for they shall have their fill.
> Blessed are the merciful, for they shall receive mercy.
> Blessed are the pure of heart, for they shall see God.
> Blessed are the peacemakers, for they shall be called sons of God.
> Blessed are those who are persecuted for doing God's will, for theirs is the kingdom of heaven.
> Blessed are you when they insult you and persecute you and say every sort of evil thing against you on account of me; rejoice and be glad, because your reward will be great in heaven" (5:3–12).

Jesus' logic is upside down. According to us, it is blessed to be rich, beautiful, healthy, and powerful. It is blessed to be honored and recognized. For Jesus, instead, it is blessed to be poor,[2] afflicted, meek, hungry, suffer-

---

2. Luke says, "Blessed are the poor," while Matthew adds "in spirit," giving us to understand that the poverty of which he speaks is humility. The ecumenical version of the Bible translates it: "Blessed those who are poor before God." Jesus explains the meaning of this beatitude in the following chapter, when he will invite us to be like the birds in the sky (Mt 6:25–34).

ing, a peacemaker.... These are two opposing ways of seeing and judging things. The criterion God uses to value and judge reality is diametrically opposed to that of the world.

The word Jesus uses to designate the position of blessedness (*makàrios* in Greek, *ahsrè* in Hebrew) expresses a profound happiness, the joy at the foundation of existence, which comes from God.[3] The term "happy" differs from "blessed" (*euloghemènos* in Greek and *barùk* in Hebrew) and cannot be equated to categories of human happiness. In fact, the Greek uses the word *eudàimon* for the joy one obtains from a satisfactory human living, the joy of the senses and of friendship. Therefore the blessed are not simply those who are content or who are fortunate. On the mountain Jesus gives place above all to freedom, to the joy of those who succeed in seeing things from another perspective, that of God and of his Reign. It is a strange joy according to the logic of the world, but a real joy for those who, like Jesus, await the coming of God and his justice.[4]

There is no excuse instead for our laziness and injustice. If the Master calls the poor blessed, it is not so that the rich can rest easy, as Luke explains well in his list of "woes": "But woe to you rich, for you have your delights"

---

3. In the Bible, we find this cry of happiness fifty-two times, of which twenty-six are in the Psalms.

4. The most noticeable thing in this sequence of the Beatitudes are the motivations, introduced by *hòti,* "for, because." These define Jesus' precise viewpoint, which is decisively eschatological, open to the future of God: "for they shall be consoled [by God], for they shall inherit the earth [according to the promise of God]," and so forth.

(Lk 6:24). Jesus' cry is equivalent to an explosive and subversive charge. Only if we turn our criteria of values—clearly unjust in the eyes of God—upside down will there be a livable and beautiful world, because it will be based on fraternity and solidarity.

Eight times a "beatitude" rings out in unchanging pattern, expressed in the third person plural, and therefore addressed to all those who find themselves in the situations mentioned: "poor in spirit, afflicted, meek...."

We asked earlier for whom the Sermon on the Mount was intended. We can already respond that the first eight beatitudes are formulated in a way that embraces and involves not only the disciples, but all those who in the course of the centuries concretely find themselves in categories of the poor and the meek, of the humble, of the afflicted and the suffering....

But in the ninth beatitude there is a change of form. One notices a direct appeal to "you," searching for those who are closer. I imagine Jesus shifting his gaze; if before he was looking out over the crowd, now he focuses directly on those who are seated at his feet, his disciples. *Blessed are you.* And why? What does Jesus promise to those who follow him? Nothing other than the sharing of his destiny, and therefore the joy of being, with him and like him, participants in a fate that certainly is not a happy one in the world's eyes: "Blessed are you when they insult you and persecute you and say every evil thing against you...."

One can read between the lines what the disciples' condition would have been at the time of Matthew; it was a

Church in a situation of adversity and persecution because of the faith. The Jews who believed in Jesus were being insulted and persecuted by their own brothers. Such encouragement to his audience of disciples seems premature at the outset of Jesus' teaching ministry. The wording clearly reveals the hand of the evangelist, who focuses on and develops the eighth beatitude, supplementing it with a special consolation and promise for the disciples who share Jesus' destiny.

You are salt, you are light

The discourse continues in the direct form introduced with the ninth beatitude. In the foreground is the ecclesial "you," represented by the circle of disciples. Having declared them "blessed" when they find that they share his destiny (or rather persecution) and that of the prophets before him, and keeping his gaze fixed on them, the Master now shows the positive side of that experience: being salt of the earth and light of the world, a city on the mountain and a lamp shining on its lamp stand.

> "You are the salt of the earth, but if the salt should lose its taste, what can it be salted with? It is good for nothing but to be thrown outside and be trampled underfoot.
>
> "You are the light of the world. A city cannot be hidden, if it is set atop a mountain. Nor do you light a lamp and set it beneath a bushel; you set it on the lamp stand, instead, so it gives light to everyone in the house. Let your light so shine before men that they will see your good works and glorify your Father in heaven" (5:13–16).

At first glance Jesus' logic might seem to make us losers, but in reality it makes us truly "Church," that eschatological community of salvation that Jesus had in mind: *you* are the salt of the earth, *you* are the light of the world. A ton of insipid salt is not worth a pinch of real salt. It is a question of quality, not quantity.

Light, if it is enkindled, cannot but illuminate! What then is the duty of the disciples/the Church? They are called to witness to the truth and beauty of the Gospel before this crowd that, although fascinated by the Master's teaching, is not yet determined to follow him in such a way that they might pass from amazement to discipleship.

It is a matter of fascination, of a brilliant light that attracts. Matthew's Jesus insists that beautiful works (*ta kalà èrga*) are more important that beautiful words. This points to the aesthetic of the good, to the strong attraction of a luminous life. It is not a matter of acting so as to be seen, something discouraged by the Master immediately following the discourse, but rather of being authentic lights, resplendent with sanctity. Why? Because ethical beauty, no less than physical beauty, exercises an irresistible fascination; it captures the gaze and desire of those who observe it, even of unbelievers.

Dialoguing with the Word

• Stay on the mountain at the feet of Jesus, allowing the Word to illuminate the dark areas of your life and make you completely luminous.

> • Let yourself be "salted" by the Divine Master, who
> wants to cure and heal you. Make your own the
> prayer of John Henry Newman: "Stay with me, and I
> will begin to shine as you shine; to shine to the point
> of becoming a light for others. The light, O Jesus,
> will come completely from you; nothing will be my
> own merit. It will be you who shine through me on
> others."[5]

Not to abolish but to fulfill

We stop now at an important passage that throws light
on the connection between the prologue and the body of
the discourse. It continues in the direct form of the ninth
beatitude, challenging the ecclesial "you" ("do not think"),[6]
yet also establishing the principle that forms the basis of six
successive examples with "You have heard that it was said
[to the ancients]...but I say to you..." (5:21–48).

For us the answer to the text's question of how the mission of Jesus compares with that of Moses and the
prophets is self-evident, but it must have sparked a lively

---

5. Cf. J. H. Newman, *Meditations and Devotions* (London-New York-
Bombay 1907), 365.

6. The formula "Do not think that I have come" is present only in
Matthew and has an interesting parallel in 10:34: "Do not think that I
have come to spread peace on the earth; I came not to spread peace but
the sword." Similar expressions regarding the mission of Jesus with
"not...but" are found in 9:13 and 20:28.

response in Matthew's community.[7] And the Master seems to safeguard himself from any possible misunderstanding:

> "Do not think *that I came* to overturn the Torah or the Prophets; I came not to destroy, but to fulfill. For amen, *I say to you*, until the heavens and the earth pass away, not one iota or one stroke of a letter will be dropped from the Torah, until everything has come to pass" (5:17–18).

The text evinces an "I" expressed with an incontrovertible tone ("Do not think that I..."). It is the *authoritative I* of the Master who will make himself heard throughout the entire discourse ("but I say to you"), and which here is pronounced above all on the meaning of his own mission. The verb "to come" means in fact the mission of Jesus as the Messiah. "Are you he who is *to come,*" John will send others to ask from prison, "or are we to expect another?" (Mt 11:3). Now the one who is seated on the mountain and teaches with such authority declares to have come *"not to abolish"* the Law of Moses,[8] *"but to bring it to fulfillment."* In

---

7. Is the ancient Law still binding after the coming of Jesus? The problem is a serious one, but it is not easy to establish the outlines of it: disagreements between the conservative community of Palestine, and the more liberal Hellenistic community? Arguments between Pharisaic Judaism, attached to the Law of Moses, and anarchistic Greek Christianity, which felt itself liberated from the Law? It is difficult to answer such questions regarding how the texts came about.

8. The formula "Law and Prophets" signifies the whole of Scripture according to a bipartite subdivision, present also in Rom 3:21 and frequently in Mt: 7:12; 11:13; 22:40. Instead it is rather rare in Judaism, where the three-party subdivision is common: Law, Prophets, Writings (similar to Lk 24:44: Law, Prophets, and Psalms).

what way? By radically interpreting it according to love, as is apparent in the examples that follow.

Jesus "fulfills" the Law not only because he follows it, but because he shows its full realization, while tracing it back to its sources, or rather to the fundamental requirements that should attend it: love of God and love of neighbor. With Jesus' coming, Scripture does not lose its normative character, but the norm is decidedly reinforced toward love, outlined in the golden rule: "Therefore, whatever you want others to do for you, do so for them as well; for this is the Torah and the Prophets" (7:12).

When all is said and done, Jesus fulfills the Law by breaking open all the prophetic meanings it contains.

The most Jewish verse

Matthew 5:18 has been labeled the most Jewish verse in the whole New Testament. Of the previous binomial (the Law and the Prophets) it mentions only the stability of the Law. Nothing will be taken away from it, not even the smallest sign, such as the *iota* (*yod*) and the *apostrophe*, that is, the smallest signs in the Hebraic writing system.[9]

What is the meaning of this affirmation and how is it interpreted in line with the last page of Matthew, where Risen One's word will knock down not merely one iota but will completely overturn the Law requiring circumcision: "Whoever believes and is baptized will be saved"?

---

9. *Iota* is the corresponding Greek to the Hebrew *yod*. Is this an implicit reference to Matthew's "Greek audience"?

Evidently the evangelist was motivated by a problem that must have been very real within his community. Such is not the case for us today, even if the problem of the relationship between the Law and the Spirit still remains. In effect, 5:18 could also be interpreted in the same way, that is, in the sense that the letter is useful in maintaining a "spirit" that is not allowed to slip but is brought to fulfillment. I like the story that rabbis recount of a dialogue that takes place in heaven between the Book of Deuteronomy and the Lord of the world. In it, Deuteronomy complains to the Eternal Father because Solomon has dared to break the Law by breaking only one *yod* (iota):

"Who accuses Solomon?"

Rabbi Jehoshua ben Levi said, "The Yod in *yarbeh.*"

Rabbi Simeone ben Jokai thought, "The book of Deuteronomy went up to heaven, prostrated itself before God and said: Lord of the world, you have written in your law: whoever violates only one prescription of any testament violates the whole of it. And here Solomon is trying to destroy one of my yods..."

And God answered, "Solomon and thousands like him will pass away, but not even one yod in you will pass away."

This story illustrates the perennial validity of the Law which remains "stable," contrary to Solomon who instead will pass away, as will every other mortal.[10] The story is speaking of the Hebrew text of Deuteronomy 17:17,

---

10. The story, from the Midrash on Leviticus, repeated in the Midrash on the Song of Songs, is cited by H. Hendrickx, *The Sermon on the Mount* (London: Chapman, 1984), 48.

which reads: *lo' yarbèh-lo nashìm* = "he [the king] must not acquire many wives for himself," while Solomon did precisely the contrary. In this case what does it mean to break one *yod*, the smallest letter in the Hebrew alphabet? It means to break the original spirit along with it—even more, to twist and distort its meaning! What should have been the supporting principle for a monogamous law thus became a justification for polygamy!

"Until the heavens and the earth pass away"

Is the Law then destined to remain forever? The divine Master affirms that it is destined to last "until the heavens and the earth pass away, until everything has come to pass" (5:18)—an apocalyptic expression we find also in Luke 16:17: "But it is easier for the heavens and the earth to pass away than for one stroke of a letter to fall from the Torah." These strong statements recall an apocalyptic feature that Matthew underscores in his account of Jesus' death. After the sign of the ripping of the Temple veil from top to bottom, recorded also by the other two synoptic Gospels, only Matthew includes that "the earth was shaken and the rocks were torn apart, and the tombs were opened and many bodies of the saints who had fallen asleep arose, and they came out of the tombs after his resurrection and went into the holy city and appeared to many people" (27:52–53).

All of this seems to hint of end times. The resurrection of the dead is in fact expected at the end, as the beginning of the new world. "I believe in the resurrection of the dead and life everlasting," we affirm in the Profession of Faith.

Jesus' death puts an end to the preceding economy of salvation based on the Law, of which the Temple was the expression. If the veil in the Temple, which kept the divine presence hidden, is ripped open, then the earth also is rent and the dead are raised. These are ambivalent signs referring us to end times and new beginnings, after which everything "has been fulfilled."

And so this exacting verse is meant to describe the mission itinerary of Jesus, who himself freely submitted to the Law in order to carry it, through the gift of himself, to the complete fulfillment of love.

A greater justice

We have digressed a little into the account of Jesus' death and resurrection in order to find the key to the verse recognized as the "most Jewish" in the entire New Testament. Now, however, we return to the mountain where Jesus declares to his disciples that they will need a greater justice in order "to enter" the Kingdom:

> "For I tell you, unless your righteousness greatly exceeds that of the scribes and Pharisees, you will never enter into the kingdom of heaven" (5:20).

Here, the term "justice" (*dikaiosynê*) means right behavior and is connected to the Law. What is in question, however, is not the idea of justice but its *measure*. The Master is declaring the justice of the scribes and Pharisees (not that of the poor) *insufficient*.[11] And it is understood imme-

---

11. J. Gnilka, *Il Vangelo di Matteo,* I, 229.

diately that this is not without importance for the subject of the discourse.

Insufficient is the measure of the official interpreters of the Law (the scribes) and also that of the strict observers of it (the Pharisees). Why? "The scribes and Pharisees," the Master will say later on, "sit on the chair of Moses, so do and observe whatever they tell you, but do not imitate their actions, for they do not do what they say" (23:2–3).

Does the greater justice have to do with consistency? Undoubtedly, but it must first of all be based on the hermeneutic of love. Jesus keeps to what Moses "has said" and goes beyond it, because the measure of superabundant justice is the same perfection/mercy of the Father: "So you be perfect as your heavenly Father is perfect" (5:48).

Jesus stirs the conscience of the community

The Master therefore criticizes the righteousness of the scribes and Pharisees, but he does not refer to them specifically as he will later in Jerusalem: "But woe to you, scribes and Pharisees, you hypocrites! You shut the door to the kingdom of heaven in men's faces—you are not going in, but you will not allow those who *are* trying to enter to go in" (23:13; the text continues until v. 31).

Instead, on the mountain of Galilee "you" describes the disciples, the circle of those seated around Jesus' feet and completely absorbed in listening to him—in a word, the Church. It is to us that Jesus addresses the warning: "Unless *your* righteousness greatly exceeds...you will never enter into the Kingdom of heaven"!

And at this point on the mountain a series of opposites resounds: "You have heard it said...but I say to you" (5:21–48). Is Jesus here setting himself against the Law? In reality, what at first hearing sounds like "antithesis" is not confirmation that Jesus opposes the biblical Law, but that he interprets it in a more profound way than the scribes and Pharisees do. He interprets the Law based on the requirements of love, showing the "greater" justice and righteousness needed to enter the Kingdom:

— reconciliation instead of murder and anger (vv. 21–26);

— self-control instead of adultery and scandal (vv. 27–30);

— mutual fidelity instead of rejection (vv. 31–32);

— truth and straightforwardness instead of taking oaths (vv. 33–37);

— relinquishing violence instead of nurturing vengeance (vv. 38–42);

— love for one's enemies instead of hatred (vv. 43–48).

Remember the formula that introduces these six examples. Jesus does not say: "It was written," but, "You have heard that it was said." The confrontation is not directly with Scripture but with the *Toràh she be al pe* ("the spoken Law"), the oral tradition that comes from and follows the Scriptures as an interpretation of the same. "It was said" does not refer only to Moses, but to the uninterrupted chain of interpreters and teachers who have spoken and continue to speak the divine Word to the people (especially in the liturgical context) and interpret its meaning. The Master's authoritative "I" resounds in the context of a living tradition that he makes use of and exceeds, toward the greater righteousness that allows one to enter the King-dom.

Jesus dreams of a community that is neither satisfied with repeating what "was said" nor with merely observing what "was written," but that is open to accepting the deep-er meaning to which the spirit of the Law invites us, according to the Father's loving measure.

"Go first and be reconciled!"

The ardent hope of Jesus, as well as of the evangelist Matthew, was that when the Gospel was written, the dan-ger to which we modern Christians are unfortunately accustomed would have been avoided: that of a liturgy that goes ahead peacefully, satisfied with following the ritual while being unconcerned about whether life is in harmony with what is being celebrated. Matthew, instead, has the courage to propose the interruption of the ritual for those Christians who during the liturgical offertory are aware that something isn't right (5:23–24). And not because you have intentionally offended your brother, but because he perhaps might have something to say about you if you give him the occasion.

And so the first "but I say to you" voiced by Jesus coun-terposes the urgency of reconciliation to murder and hatred:

> "You have heard that it was said to the ancients: *You shall not murder,* and that whoever does commit murder shall be liable to judgment. But I say to you that anyone who is angry with his brother shall be liable to judgment, and who-ever says to his brother, 'Raqa!' shall be liable to the

Sanhedrin, and whoever says, 'You fool!' shall be liable to the fire of Gehenna.

"So if you are presenting your offering at the altar and remember there that your brother has something against you, leave your offering there before the altar and first go be reconciled with your brother, and then you can come and make your offering. Come to terms quickly with your opponent while you are on your way with him, or your opponent may hand you over to the judge, and the judge to the guard, and you will be thrown into prison. Amen, I say to you, you will not come out of there until you pay back the last penny" (5:21–26).

I limit myself to just a few highlights. The fifth commandment demands that we do not kill, as the first and fundamental recognition of the right of the other and of a person's supreme good, life. This is the rock-solid foundation and basis of love toward the other. Murder, therefore, is considered a crime and strictly condemned by Mosaic Law (and not only by it). But is it enough not to violate the fifth commandment in order to give God the worship he deserves? Jesus goes beyond the demands of justice, asking for a respect of the other that even avoids anger and its consequences. In his eyes, the one who insults a brother or sister is paradoxically worthy of a condemnation even more serious than murder. The surprising escalation of condemnation is noted: judgment in court, judgment before the Sanhedrin (the highest Jewish religious authority), and the fire of Gehenna! The paradox is meant to illustrate an element we risk passing over: that anger clouds our reason and separates us from compassion to the point of killing another in one's own heart (cf. 1 Jn 3:15).

The second part of the passage shows how liturgy and life should go together. It is not enough not to kill anyone in order to offer worship pleasing to God. Jesus opens the demands of justice to a broader viewpoint, one of authentic communion. Therefore, if in the liturgical setting your heart opportunely awakens your conscience, telling you that your brother or sister has serious reasons for bringing legal action against you (as the text immediately following, which speaks of courts, leads us to understand), you do well to interrupt the ritual to go first and be reconciled.

No to adultery and its desires

The second "but I say to you" places the greater justice within the sphere of the closest relationships, those having to do with the life of married couples:

> "You have heard that it was said, *You shall not commit adultery,* but I say to you that anyone who looks at a woman with lust for her has already committed adultery with her in his heart.
>
> "If your right eye causes you to sin, pull it out and throw it away from you! It is better for you to lose one part of your body than to have the whole body thrown into Gehenna. And if your right hand causes you to sin, cut it off and throw it away from you! It is better for you to lose one part of your body than to have your whole body go off to Gehenna" (5:27–30).

Jesus connects the sixth and ninth commandments, which respectively prohibit adultery and the desire for it. He takes this position within the framework of family rights and ownership at the time, which explains why his remark is typically directed to men, as if for women the possibility of this kind of sin—that is, to look at a man and desire him—did not even exist.

How do things stand in the Bible? Although both a man and a woman could be accused of adultery (Lev 20:10), the commandment is addressed only to men, whether in Exodus 20:14 or in Deuteronomy 5:18. In this context the woman occupies first place in the list of "goods" belonging to a man (cf. Ex 20:17), for which reason adultery or the desire for it corresponds to the violation of the "rights of ownership."

One understands then why the greater righteousness that the Master proposes here directly concerns "men." Jesus' viewpoint is in perfect agreement with the beatitude of the "pure of heart." Not only must one avoid adultery, condemned by the Law and by society, but adulterous desires must also be shunned. In other words, what should be avoided is not merely visible and condemnable social evil, but also that which contaminates the heart, which kills the beauty and truth of love.

Jesus speaks in images, with figurative language and a love of paradox that is dear to Semitics: it is better to tear out an eye or cut off a hand than to perish completely! This parabolic language can be understood only within the broader framework of the faith and hope that introduce the Beatitudes. Viewed from a self-centered and worldly perspective, none of this makes any sense, but if we share the eschatological hope of Jesus, we understand what his words are leading up to. "This way of loving is so precious that, if necessary, one should be willing to give up even one's right eye or right hand rather than renounce it."[12]

Not rejection but fidelity

With the third "but I say to you," Jesus places against the practice of divorce (a male privilege) the greater righteousness of faithful love:

"And it was said, *Whoever puts his wife away must give her a written notice of divorce.* But I say to you, anyone who puts his wife away—except by reason of an unlawful union—makes her an adulteress, and whoever marries a divorced woman commits adultery" (5:31–32).

Here also the Master seems to be addressing only men. While affirming the indissolubility of matrimony, he pronounces in favor of women, the weaker party when it came to family rights. At that time, in fact, divorce was a completely masculine privilege. According to the formula for divorce reported in the Mishnah, the man said to the woman: "Receive from me a decree of divorce, a letter of repudiation, and a document that says you are free to marry whom you want" (Git IX, 3). But Jesus contests this practice, examining two cases: the rejection of the wife and marriage to a repudiated woman.

On the theme of indissoluble matrimony, except in the case of *pornéia*, Jesus will return in 19:3–9 in open debate with the Pharisees. In that context, he will again affirm his position even more explicitly, going back to the Creator's

---

12. Giavini, *Ma io vi dico,* 83.

original plan: no longer two but only one flesh, for which reason man should not separate what God has joined together.[13] Also in this context, Matthew (and only he) makes reference to the case of *pornéia*. What is this about? The Greek Bible of the seventies uses *pornéia* to translate the Hebrew term *zenunìm* or *taznût*, which can mean "prostitution" in a sexual context (Gen 38:24; Hos 1:2) and "idolatry" in a religious context (Ezek 23:11:29; Hos 2:6; 4:12; 5:4).

But what is the meaning of the term as it is used in Matthew? The answer is decisive if we are to understand Jesus' position in the Jewish debate of the Temple of his day. If the term means a woman prostitute, then Jesus aligns himself with the thinking of the school of Shammai, a rabbi of the first century, rather than with a radical interpretation of the Law as in the preceding antithesis. The suspicion arises immediately that this is not the case, that *pornéia* can mean something else, as in Leviticus 18:6–18, where it means the illicit union between blood relations, and in 1 Corinthians 5:1, where Paul deals with the case of incest.[14]

---

13. The passage is noted also in the other two synoptics: Mk 10:2–12 and Lk 16:18. On this argument, see: H. Balthensweiler, *Il matrimonio nel Nuovo Testamento* (Brescia: Paideia, 1981); C. Marucci, *Parole di Gesù sul divorzio* (Naples: Mocelliana, 1982).

14. Cf. E. Vallauri, "Le clausole matteane ul divorzio. Tendenze esegetiche recenti," *Laurentianum* 17 (1976), 82–112; B. Witherington, "Matthew 5:32 and 19:9—Exception or Exceptional Situation?" *New Testament Studies* 31 (1985), 571–576; C. Marucci, "Clausole mattenae e critica testuale. In merito alla teoria di H. Crouzel sul testo originale di Mt 19:9," *Rivista Biblica* 38 (1990), 301–325.

However things stand, from the stance we are taking of community and mission, one thing remains clear: the community that Jesus imagined is based on loyalty and faithfulness in love, starting with that primary unit which is the married couple, according to the original design of God.

Simply yes or no

The fourth antithesis addresses the custom of valuing a word given in oath:

> "Again you have heard that it was said to your ancestors, *You shall not break your oaths* and, *You shall fulfill your oaths to the Lord.* But I tell you not to swear at all, neither by heaven, because it is the throne of God, nor by earth, because it is the footstool for his feet, nor by Jerusalem, because it is the city of the great King, nor shall you swear by your head, because you are not able to make one hair white or black. Let your 'yes' be 'yes' and your 'no' be 'no'; anything more than that is from the Evil One" (5:33–37).

Jesus' argument stems from two biblical instructions: the warning against perjury (Lev 19:12; Ex 20:7) and the obligation to fulfill oaths (Num 30:3; Deut 23:22). "Offer to God a sacrifice of thanksgiving, and pay your vows [oaths] to the Most High," says Psalm 50:14.

The practice of taking oaths was very common. Jesus will later attack the scribes and Pharisees for the hypocrisy with which they interpret the encumbrance of oaths:

> "Woe to you, blind guides, who say, 'Whoever swears by the sanctuary, that is nothing, but whoever swears by the gold of the sanctuary is bound.' You are foolish and blind! For what is greater, the gold or the sanctuary that sanctifies the gold?

And, 'Whoever swears by the altar, that is nothing, but whoever swears by the offering upon it is bound.' You are blind!
For what is greater, the offering on the altar or the altar that
sanctifies the offering? Therefore, whoever swears by the
altar swears by the altar and also by everything on it, and
whoever swears by the sanctuary swears by the sanctuary and
also by the One who dwells within, and whoever swears by
heaven swears by the throne of God and also by the One
seated upon it" (23:16–22).

Jesus takes a definite position regarding the practice of
oaths, warning against it without exception. Philo of
Alexandria, a Jew of Greek culture from the first century,
will also recognize that "to not swear at all is a magnificent
attitude, very useful in life."[15] But why shouldn't God be
dragged into a situation; why shouldn't one swear at all?
Because human relations should be based on honesty and
sincerity, on open and straightforward speaking guided by
trust.

That this teaching of the Master had a profound echo
in the Judeo-Christian area is also attested to by a passage
from the Letter of James: "Above all, my brothers, do not
swear, whether by heaven, earth, or some other oath; let
your 'yes' be 'yes' and your 'no' be 'no,' lest you come under
condemnation" (5:12).[16]

---

15. *De decalogo,* 84; according to Josephus Flavius, the Essenes also
abstain from taking oaths (*Bell. Iud.,* II, 8, 6).

16. P. Minear, "Yes or No: the Demand for Honesty in the Early
Church," *Novum Testamentum* 13 (1971), 1–13.

Do not resist the evildoer

With the fifth "but I say to you," Jesus goes beyond the law of "an eye for an eye," to a justice that seeks not only to limit vengeance but also to bring back the violent one:

"You have heard that it was said: *An eye for an eye and a tooth for a tooth.* But I tell you not to resist the evildoer; on the contrary, if anyone strikes you on the right cheek, turn the other to him as well; if anyone wants to go to law with you and take your tunic, give him your cloak as well, and if anyone forces you to go one mile, go with him for two. Give to those who ask of you, and do not reject those who wish to borrow from you" (5:38–42).

Beyond the formulation, which sounds brutal to our ears ("an eye for an eye and a tooth for a tooth"), the *jus talionis* was a way of containing violence through *proportionality:* to every wound there must correspond a pain equal to it. In effect it was like saying: *You are not to exceed a certain boundary in your right to carry out justice; contain your desire for retaliation.* It opposed the logic of vengeance found in someone like Lamech, who declared with pride: "I have killed a man for wounding me, a young man for striking me. If Cain is avenged sevenfold, truly Lamech seventy-sevenfold" (Gen 4:23–24).

With respect to such vindictive logic, the law of retaliation is a considerable affirmation of civility. Even if it does not pertain to the specific patrimony of Israel (we already find it, in fact, in the Code of Hammurabi, in the second millennium B.C.), it undoubtedly constitutes a fundamental principle of Old Testament legislation.[17] But Jesus decisively takes another viewpoint. Rather than reestablish order and justice through the use of violence, he proposes a different strategy, the end of which is the pedagogical recovery of the aggressor and of the violent. It is a demanding strategy, ready even to renounce one's own rights.[18]

It is the way of forgiveness and non-violence, in agreement with the greater justice that allows one to enter the Kingdom. The Master delivers his teaching with three examples of brutal violence: the slap on the right cheek, the compensation of the cloak, and military coercion.

A slap was something particularly offensive in ancient times, so much so that the Mishnah provided a more serious penalty for it than for the use of one's fist (BQ 8:6). Jesus proposes that a person offer the other cheek to one's aggressor not out of craziness, much less out of pride or cynicism. The image alludes above all to the Servant of the Lord, who does not oppose the violence of those who persecute and strike him (Isa 50:6; 53:4–7), as Jesus does not defend himself in his passion (Mt 26:67; 1 Pt 2:21–23).

---

17. Cf. Ex 21:24; Lev 24:20; Deut 19:21. At the time of Jesus, there were many who attempted to overcome this principle, for example, the community of Qumran which had banished vengeance from its midst: "I will not repay to anyone the evil they have done me, I will repay with goodness" (*Rules*, 10:17).

18. Cf. G. Theissen, "La rinuncia alla violenza, l'amore per il nemico (Mt 5:38–48; Lk 6:27–38) e il loro sfondo sociale," in Id., *Sociologico del cristianesimo primitivo* (Genoa: Marietti, 1987), 142–175.

The second example refers to a judicial lawsuit over one's tunic, the daytime dress that was worn directly over the skin and that could be requested as compensation for damages. Jesus suggests that retaliation take the form of giving to the contender not only one's coat but also one's cloak—an item that absolutely could not be taken, because it was not only a poor person's garment but also his "shelter": "If you take your neighbor's cloak in pawn, you shall restore it before the sun goes down; for it may be your neighbor's only clothing to use as cover; in what else shall that person sleep?" (Ex 22:26).

What is the meaning of this paradoxical logic? There is a measure of wickedness, the Master seems to say, that one can hope to overcome only by renouncing one's rights![19]

In the same way we move to the third example, being forced to walk for a mile. This is referring to a type of military coercion as happened to Simon of Cyrene, who was coming back from the fields when he "was forced" to carry the cross of Jesus (cf. 27:32).

The last sentence invites one not to turn one's back on the poor who ask to borrow (cf. Deut 15:7–11). But it also asks one to renounce one's own rights within the same logic of love. The point is not to take the examples to the letter, but to accept the spirit and objective that the indi-

---

19. The philosopher Diogenes Laerzio recommends the same thing: "To the one who asks for your tunic, give him also your cloak," cited by Gnilka, *Il Vangelo di Matteo,* I, 277. There is a Latin proverb that says: "To the one who takes you to court for an egg, give him the chicken as well."

cated strategy means to follow: to disarm the violent person with a superabundant measure of goodness.[20]

Love also for one's enemies

With the sixth "but I say to you," the discourse reaches its peak; in reality, the command to love one's enemies constitutes the summit of Jesus' ethics:

> "You have heard that it was said: *Love your neighbor and hate your enemy.* But I say to you, love your enemies, and pray for those who persecute you, so that you will become sons of your Father in heaven, because he causes his sun to rise on the evil and the good, and rain to fall on the just and the unjust. For if you love those who love you, what rewards will you have? Do not even the tax collectors do the same? And if you greet only your brothers, what great thing are you doing? Do not even the Gentiles do the same? So be perfect as your heavenly Father is perfect" (5:43–48).

For the sixth time those who have heard the Master are sent back to what they had previously heard. But where in the Bible do we find it said to hate the enemy? Biblical scholars have had some difficulty in documenting this "you have heard it said," which Jesus takes for granted. In fact, while there is a clear command in the Bible to love one's neighbor (cf. Lev 19:18), there is, strictly speaking,

---

20. For example, when Jesus is brutally struck before the Sanhedrin, he does not react in Matthew (26–67), but in John it doesn't happen that he offers the other cheek. Certainly, no one would ever imagine him throwing bolts of lightning at his tormentors; instead, he would have looked into their eyes and said with disarming meekness, "If I have spoken wrongly, bear witness against the wrong, but if I have spoken rightly, why do you hit me?" (Jn 18:23).

not one to hate one's enemy. There are, however, places where it is not easy to separate the two concepts; where there is a superimposition taking place between the enemies of God and those of the people, such as in the *cursing psalms*. One recalls Psalm 137, a masterpiece of poetry and emotion, which begins with the complaint of those who have been deported—"By the rivers of Babylon... there we sat down and there we wept when we remembered Zion"—and ends with a vehement request for vengeance:

Remember, O LORD, against the Edomites
the day of Jerusalem's fall,
how they said, "Tear it down! Tear it down!
Down to its foundations!"
O daughter of Babylon, you devastator!
Happy shall they be who pay you back
what you have done to us!
Happy shall they be who take your little ones
and dash them against the rock! (Ps 137:7–9)

This double "happy they," full of atrocious violence, is striking! Hatred of one's enemies was also cultivated at Qumran, where the members were called to "love all the children of light, each one destined in the assembly of God, but to hate all the children of the shadows, each one whose fault put them under God's vengeance" (1QS 1, 9s).

It seems that the greater justice of Jesus is set against this reasoning that presumptuously anticipates the divine judgment, separating the children of the shadows (the infidels and evil ones) from those of the light (the elect). One needs to love not only one's neighbor and one's brother/

sister in the faith, but even the adversary of God and of his Church. Jesus proposes a broadening of position, directly appealing to the God of creation who by his behavior shows that he loves not only the good but also the wicked. His sun, in fact, rises on everyone without prejudice.

On this experience, as positive as it is universal, Jesus bases the principle rooted in his ethics: the *imitation of God.* "Love your enemies, and pray for those who persecute you, so that you will become sons of your Father," he concludes, presenting filial relationship with God as a work in progress, as in the seventh beatitude. The face of God will shine on the men and women throughout history who in the day of tribulation and violence have sown forgiveness and compassion, or rather love, which is stronger than hate or death: "Blessed are the peacemakers, for they shall be called sons of God" (5:9).

Those capable of loving their enemies show themselves to be sons (creatures) of God, because parentage is recognized by similarity. In other words, it is not only being—existence that is received and creaturely—that is important, but also the ethical-existential becoming; what you yourself do; that face you are giving yourself through the exercise of your freedom and through your choices of love or hate, egoism or concern for life. In this sense, sonship becomes a way of imitation.[21]

---

21. At the foundation of this teaching one is aware of the echo of biblical wisdom: "Be a father to orphans, and be like a husband to their mother; you will then be like a son of the Most High, and he will love you more than does your mother," exhorts Sirach (4:10).

The theme is dear also to stoicism and in particular to Seneca: "If you want to imitate the gods, do good works also to the ungrateful, because even on the wicked the sun rises and the sea is open also to pirates."[22] There is also a Buddhist text that reads: "If you do not practice compassion toward your enemy, toward whom will you practice it?"[23]

It is hard to escape the fascination of Jesus' ethics, which propose an alternative logic even at the social level.

Dialoguing with the Word

- Allow yourself to be challenged by the demanding "but I say to you" of Jesus, who proposes the greater justice inspired by charity: "Be perfect as your heavenly Father is perfect." How does one live this call to holiness in the following of Jesus?

- It is well known that Gandhi was fascinated by the teaching of Jesus. When Gandhi was asked why he didn't become a Christian, he responded: "Because there are millions of Christians who don't live as Christians." What about you? Do you witness to the values of reconciliation, forgiveness, and non-violence proposed and lived by Jesus?

---

22. Cited in Gnilka, *Il Vangelo di Matteo,* I, 291.

23. *Compendio delle Pratiche,* cited by the Dalai Lama, which goes along with the Gospel text: "It is very important to maintain a correct attitude toward one's own enemies. If one succeeds in cultivating a positive attitude, enemies become the best spiritual teachers because their presence offers the possibility of growing in and developing tolerance, patience, and understanding. The analogy expressed in the Gospel—'the sun does not make a difference on whom it shines'—is very significant. The sun shines on everyone and does not discriminate. It is a wonderful metaphor of compassion. It gives us a sense of its all-encompassing nature," *Incontro con Gesù: Una lettera buddista del Vangelo* (Milan: Mondadori, 1998), 19–20.

Religion without ostentation

Jesus' discourse seems to end with the invitation to become sons of the Father who is good and generous toward all, and to be "perfect" as he is. But the Master prolongs his stay on the mountain and continues with his catechesis. Now he develops the theme of greater justice with regard to the three fundamental religious practices: almsgiving, prayer, and fasting (6:1–18).

Jesus does not call into question what we read in the Book of Tobit: "Prayer with fasting is good, but better than both is almsgiving with righteousness" (12:8). He does not argue the goodness of these practices, but addresses why and for whom they are done:

> "Take care not to perform your good deeds in front of others in order to be seen by them; if you do, you will have no reward from your Father in heaven" (6:1).

The disciples ("you") are not supposed to show off in doing good in order to receive social recognition, honor, or esteem, but must simply do what is pleasing to the Father in the firm conviction that the Father who is just and good, who sees what is hidden, in his own time "will reward you." This is the refrain that closes each of the three thematic panels and connects them in a kind of triptych: "and your Father, who sees in secret, will reward you."

A religion of the heart rather than one of outward appearance? I would say yes, but it is also a religion that does not fall into sentimentalism. In fact, the crux of the whole argument is the authentic relationship of love that must characterize religious behavior. Be careful about the vanity that threatens the very roots of religious practice, because it takes attention away from God and directs it to the ego. "How can you believe, who receive glory from each other, yet do not seek glory from God alone?" (Jn 5:44). Between faith and vanity an unyielding distance separates God from idolatry (of oneself).

Do not sound a trumpet before you when you give alms

The duty of helping the poor is proposed as a fundamental requirement of authentic religious experience.[24] But there is in fact a way of helping the poor that does not respect their dignity, therefore wounding God rather than giving him honor.

How can we stigmatize helping the poor for reasons of vanity, in order to merit the title and honor of benefactor? Jesus makes use of caricature: behold the hypocrites, the actors who strut about impressively and blow their own horn while giving their offerings!

His disciples are not to act in this way. And here Jesus shifts from the plural to the singular "you," directly challenging the individual not in order to assure the tranquility of the community, but to underscore the point that vanity pollutes personal conscience:

"Whenever you give alms, do not sound a trumpet before you, like the hypocrites do in the synagogues and in the

---

24. The ideal of the first Christian communities was the sharing of goods (Acts 2:44); Paul himself carefully organized the collection for the poor of Jerusalem and recommended avoiding the scandal of carousing next to one who was struggling just to survive (1 Cor 11:20–22).

streets so people will praise them. Amen, I say to you, they have their full reward! But when you give alms, do not let your left hand know what your right hand is doing, so that your alms may be in secret, and your Father who sees in secret will reward you" (6:2–4).

Public recognition, Jesus concludes, is the reward for your vanity. But you have lost the occasion of keeping something in store for God, the chance to give him a gift.

"One's almsgiving is like a signet-ring with the LORD, and he will keep a person's kindness like the apple of his eye," writes Jesus, son of Sirach (Sir 17:22). And Jesus of Nazareth is in full agreement with this teaching. The discretion that should accompany an act of generosity is rooted in the conviction that there is a close connection between service given to the poor and that given to God (cf. Mt 25). For this reason it should not be profaned but kept in the secret of one's heart, where one deals with the profound and filial relationship of love.

Pray to your Father in secret

The theme of prayer occupies a central place and is the longest passage in the entire discourse. It is highlighted by the fact that it contains the "Our Father," the Christian prayer par excellence, placed in the center like the pearl of greatest justice that finds its style and content in the filial relationship of Jesus with the Father.[25]

---

25. Unlike Luke, who presents the Our Father in briefer form and because of the explicit request of the disciples, who are fascinated by the prayer of the Master: see Lk 11:1–4.

The first part of the passage runs parallel with the other two sides of the triptych, disputing the caricatured practice of the "hypocrites":[26]

"And when you pray, do not be like the hypocrites. They love to pray standing in the synagogues and on the corners of wide streets, so people will notice them. Amen, I say to you, they have their full reward! But when you pray, go into your storeroom and shut the door, pray to your Father who is hidden, and your Father who sees what is hidden will reward you" (6:5–6).

Certainly the importance of prayer—which Jesus himself practiced for prolonged periods, going by himself to solitary places—is not being called into question here. Instead the Master is criticizing vanity in prayer—that is, showing off in order to obtain the recognition and esteem that would matter in a typically religious setting such as the Jewish world at the time of Jesus.

In the synagogue and other designated places, prayer was made publicly, standing upright (Neh 9:4). But here it is neither liturgical posture nor the prayerful involvement of the body that Jesus disputes, but the desire to be seen. It is as if Jesus is saying not to reduce prayer to a bodily and formal level. And above all, he is telling us not to pray with the pretext of putting ourselves on display or making a scene.

One's relationship with God should be loving, involving the whole person and aiming at intimacy. *Do not put it out*

---

26. *Hypocrite* is a term which comes from the theater: it designates the actor who hides his face behind a mask. It points out the differences between the external and the internal.

for display in the marketplace, Jesus warns us, *guard your privacy!* "Go into your room and close the door...." Prayer involves the secret chamber everyone has, the poor as well as the rich: the chamber of the heart. And in this chamber there is no need to multiply words. Love is enough.

Do not multiply words

In contrast with the negative example of the one who turns to God with many words, there is the prayer taught by Jesus, the "Our Father." It unfolds in two parts, with petitions that regard God, his holy name, and the coming of his Kingdom (vv. 9–10), and questions regarding fundamental human needs for bread, forgiveness, and deliverance from evil (vv. 11–13).

The prayer is articulated with pronouns and possessive adjectives that in the first part are in the second person singular—"*your* name," "*your* kingdom," "*your* will"—while in the second they are in the first person plural: "give *us* our bread, forgive *us* our debts, do not lead *us* into temptation, deliver *us* from evil." There are seven petitions altogether, symbolically rendering this prayer perfect and complete. Interwoven from the very first invocation are one's direct rapport with the Father (the Abba of Jesus) and the needs of humanity. Even in the secret of one's own room, the disciple of Jesus is a universal brother or sister; one is not to isolate oneself and recite "my Father" but "our Father."

Do not let others see that you are fasting

By abstaining from food and drink, the believer intends to affirm his or her total dependence on the Creator, who gives life and nourishment. At the same time, he or she expresses willingness to practice solidarity with brothers and sisters forced in ever growing numbers to go hungry because of unjust poverty. Fasting helps to purify our mind and spirit so we may hear that God wants fraternity and not social inequality; so that the goods of creation may be enjoyed by all, especially by those unjustly and continually deprived of them.[27]

But here, strictly speaking, it is neither the aspect of social justice nor dutiful solidarity with the poor that the text puts in the foreground. It is not a matter of the opportunity to fast, which Jesus himself practiced (although in a different way than the Baptist), but *why* one should fast.

With subtle irony the Master points out the vanity of the one who, fasting in order to be noticed, puts on a gloomy face:

> "When you fast, do not be gloomy like the hypocrites. They make their faces unsightly to let others see they are fasting. Amen, I say to you, they have their full reward! But when you fast, anoint your head and wash your face, so others will not see that you are fasting, but only your Father who is hidden will see, and your Father who sees what is hidden will reward you" (6:16–18).

Even fasting is a matter of love and how it should be lived, whether in relationship to God or to one's brothers and sisters. If you intend to give a gift, you wrap it up in

---

27. The meaning of fasting is being rediscovered in view of social injustice, which demands an equal distribution of the goods of the Creator. In view of this, the encounters in Assisi were developed, by invitation of John Paul II, with representatives of the various religions of the world: prayer, fasting, and solidarity with the poor.

beautiful paper and keep it as a surprise for the loved one! Similarly, do not let people see that you are fasting, but only "your Father, who sees in secret."

Finally, vanity radically threatens the purity of religious expression, transforming what was born of love for God into an affirmation of the ego. In an environment where the practice of prayer and fasting was held in great esteem, and people were therefore judged according to such parameters, Jesus reminds us that "man looks at the outward appearance, but the Lord looks on the heart" (1 Sam 16:7).[28] It is not as a Supreme Being searching the heart to terrify it, but as a good Father that God appreciates every sign of love and confirms it in the future: "he will reward you."

Freedom from worry

The discourse continues pointing out a new horizon of freedom: trust in the provident care of the Father (Mt 6:25–34). Why be afraid? Why worry? We are placed before Jesus' personal relationship with his Father and his unconditional trust, the model and parameter of the invitation to not live as though life depended on us:

> "Therefore, I tell you, do not worry about your life, what you will eat, or about your body, what you will wear. Is not life more than food and the body more than clothing? Look

---

28. This is in line with the prophet Samuel and in particular with the prophets Jeremiah and Ezekiel, who had announced during messianic times that there would come a religion of a new heart and of interiority (Jer 31:33–34; Ezek 36:27).

at the birds of the sky—they neither sow nor reap nor gather into barns, yet your heavenly Father feeds them; are you not worth more than they are? But which of you can add any time to your life by worrying? And why do you worry about clothing? Look how the lilies of the field grow; they neither work nor spin. But I tell you, even Solomon in all his glory was not arrayed like one of them. But if God so clothes the grass of the fields, which is here today and thrown into the oven tomorrow, will he not clothe you much better, O you of little faith? So do not go worrying, saying, 'What will we eat?' or, 'What will we drink?' or, 'What will we put on?' for the Gentiles seek all those things. Your heavenly Father knows you need them! But first seek the kingdom and the will of God and all those things will be given to you also. So do not go worrying about tomorrow—tomorrow will worry for itself. One day's evil is enough for a day" (6:25–34).

The passage contains a refrain that is clearly articulated four times, first as an imperative: "Do not worry!" (v. 25); then as a question: "Why do you worry?" (v. 28); and finally as persuasion: "So do not worry" (*mê merimnêsête,* vv. 31, 34).

But is it sensible to free oneself from preoccupations regarding basic needs, such as food and clothing? And how does one reach this freedom? Is it really possible to adopt the carefree manner of birds who, unlike human beings, are not worried about tomorrow? Such behavior seems improbable to concerned and responsible people facing the future.

What kind of joyful and lighthearted community is Jesus dreaming of? This carpenter's son, who understands from firsthand experience what it means to work at a trade and struggle to earn one's bread, does not seem to call into question the basic law of work, nor the social foresight and full utilization of intellectual resources needed to plan and improve the quality of life.[29]

There is a philosophical-sapiential attitude at the base of the imperative "Do not worry": the acceptance of the creature's radical dependence on the Creator, evident when faced with the unavoidable limits of death. Jesus places life and its needs (as he has already done so with prayer and fasting) beneath the loving gaze of the Father. He hands over the preoccupation of living to the very Doctor of life. It is up to God to be preoccupied with us, or rather to take care of us ahead of time, in a way that anticipates our needs and is completely dependable. It is up to the believer to simply "be occupied" with gratitude and responsibility in the present moment: "Give us this day our daily bread." Here is the antidote to the existential anxiety afflicting our days! Worrying about tomorrow (which you do not know will even come) takes away the space of freedom. It prevents you from fully living in peace and responsibility the time and the life that God gives you.

So should we all take our cue from the birds, or "the blackbirds," as Luke concretely calls them in the parallel passage? Yes, Jesus invites us to look at them and be "infected" by their freedom. He also invites us to contem-

---

29. G. De Virgilio, "Mt 6:19–34: provvidenza divina e realismo cristiano," *Rivista Biblica* 50 (2002), 3–29.

plate the flowers and allow ourselves to be surprised by their beauty. Why? Not out of some vague spirit of romanticism or ecology. If you look well, the term of comparison is not living like the birds, and neither is it the gratuitous beauty of the flowers, but the care of the Father. If God is concerned about the birds and the flowers, much more is he concerned about you. Stop worrying, therefore, and learn to trust! Be like the psalmist who sings: "I have calmed and quieted my soul, like a weaned child with its mother" (Ps 131:2).

A passage from Psalm 55 also comes to mind, which the Apostle Peter uses at the end of his first letter: "Cast all your cares on him, because he cares for you" (5:7). To liberate oneself from preoccupations is not a privilege reserved to tranquil souls; rather it is an imperative for those who are waiting and preparing for the Kingdom of God.

"Do not judge!"

The discourse continues, moving from the Father to the community (7:1–7) in order to again reinforce the theme of trust in God (7:7–11). It is as if the Christian community must breathe with two lungs, taking in the pure air of freedom from a filial relationship with God, the good Creator, and in its own time oxygenating the world with a broad exhalation of goodness.

"Do not judge," Jesus says, "and you will not be judged" (7:1). Those who judges claim the right of superiority over others and believe themselves to be better. But this right belongs only to God, before whom all are sinners and in need of mercy. This theme is also dear to St. Paul: "But this is why all you who pass judgment on others," he writes in the Letter to the Romans, "have no excuse. For to the extent that you pass judgment on others you condemn yourself, since you who judge do the very same things" (2:1).

"The disciples must not judge. If they do, they will find themselves under the judgment of God. The sword with which they condemn their brother or sister will fall on them. The cut with which they separate themselves from their neighbor, as the righteous from the unrighteous, separates them from Jesus."[30]

It goes back to the motive expressed in the Our Father, that in some way it is we ourselves who give God the measure of forgiveness and judgment: "For with the judgment you judge, you will be judged, and with the measure you measure, it will be measured out to you" (7:2).

The community of the Lord cannot claim the right of judging the world; rather they should not judge at all— whether because *krìma* (the judgment of condemnation) belongs only to God, or because one is aware that evil is not only external but internal as well. Jesus illustrates the invitation to be benevolent by using an effective hyperbole with contrasting images: "the *speck* in your brother's eye / the *log* in your own eye."

In the preceding chapter, the Master compared the eye to the lamp of the body: if the eye is healthy the whole

---

30. D. Bonhoeffer, *Sequela* (Brescia: Querininana, 1975), 161.

body is illuminated, but if the eye is diseased the body will
be in darkness (6:22–23). Now by its nature, the eye helps
one see outside and not within oneself. So the defects of
others become a mirror: what most bothers us in them
usually coincides exactly with our own defects! Therefore
benevolence hinders the temptation of considering oneself
superior to others. Only a benevolent community, one that
is patient and understanding, is able to announce in a cred-
ible way the good news of a God who forgives and cares.
Matthew will deepen this theme in the discourse on community, connecting two complementary aspects: fraternal correction and the invitation to forgive the brother
who makes a mistake—not only seven times, but always
(18:15–22).

The Golden Rule

The Master again takes up the motives of trust and
prayer. Where does one draw the strength to love and the
capacity to welcome the other as he or she is, with that
person's limitations and defects? The community has to
ask it of the Father, with insistence and complete trust, as
the greatest good:

> "Ask and it shall be given to you; seek and you shall find;
> knock and it shall be opened to you. For everyone who asks,
> will receive, and whoever seeks, will find, and to those who
> knock, it shall be opened. Or which of you, if his son asked
> for a loaf, would hand him a stone? Or if he asked for a fish,
> would hand him a snake? So if you who are evil know how
> to give good gifts to your children, all the more will your
> Father in heaven give good things to those who ask him.

Therefore, whatever you want others to do for you, do so for them as well; for this is the Torah and the Prophets" (7:7–12).

Radical love and mercy are woven together in the Sermon on the Mount. "The one who radically lives the following of Christ, living in the absolute love of God that is turned toward man in all his mercy, must consequently be merciful with everyone, and finally, even a little with himself."[31]

The house on a rock

The Sermon on the Mount concludes with an emphasis on "doing" that has nothing to do with workaholism but refers to obedient listening, which puts the Word into practice. This is how one builds one's "house" on rock:

"Therefore, everyone who hears these words of mine and acts on them is like a wise man who built his house on rock. And the rain fell and the floods came and the winds blew and beat against that house, yet it did not fall, for its foundations had been set on rock. Everyone who hears these words of mine and does not act on them is like a foolish man who built his house on sand. And the rain fell and the floods came and the winds blew and beat against that house, and it fell, and great was its fall" (7:24–27).

The house not only symbolizes a habitation, one's life and important projects (doesn't one speak of "building

31. Lohfink, *Per chi vale il Discorso della Montagna?* 97, and G. De Virgilio, "La *ekklesia* come 'società alternativa.' Ricezione dell'opera di G. Lohfink," *Rivista Biblica* 39 (1991), 467–475.

one's own life" and "constructing a family"?). To build one's own house on rock is a sign of wisdom that "pays off" in times of adversity, when the rains and the fury of the winds threaten.

The psalmist remembers that "unless the LORD builds the house, those who build it labor in vain" (Ps 127:1), and that the Lord himself is "the rock" (Ps 18:2; 95:1). In this sense Jesus concludes that only on God and with God can one's personal and communitarian life be built.

By now the sermon has reached its end. It is time to come down from the mountain in order to put into practice the Master's teaching. It is not enough to listen or simply invoke these teachings. It is not even enough to make a beautiful *lectio divina* on the Sermon on the Mount. Recognition will be based on the fruits. It is not those who fill their mouths with the praises of the Lord who will be recognized as disciples and welcomed into the Kingdom, but those who live the Golden Rule, the compendium of love. "Not everyone who says to me, 'Lord, Lord!' will enter the Kingdom of heaven; no, the one who does the will of my Father in heaven will" (7:21).

For whom is the Sermon on the Mount intended?

It is time to revisit the question raised earlier: To whom is the Sermon on the Mount addressed? Throughout a long history of interpretation, this question has been preceded by and linked with another: What really is the

Sermon on the Mount? Is it a "law," albeit "new," up-to-date, and perfected with respect to Old Testament Law? Or is it something that certainly has to do with the Law, yet not with the main purpose of displaying an ethic that humanity is incapable of observing? While the first explanation is indicative of St. Augustine's thought, the second expresses a direction once widely diffused among Protestants, appealing to the need for grace, the "law of the Spirit" of which St. Paul speaks.

Some see this wonderful sermon as highlighting the disconcerting distance between Church living and the program pointed out by Christ, allowing for a decisive change of horizon: from imminent waiting for the Kingdom of God, which characterized the eschatology of Jesus and of the first Christian communities, to its problematic delay. The radical ethic proposed in the Sermon on the Mount is understandable only in the tension of the last hour, of one who believes the end is imminent!

Historical exegesis notes, moreover, that the Sermon on the Mount has long been used to justify a double moral standard: one for the "perfect disciple" (i.e., the religious man or woman), called to follow more radical standards, and one for the laity, who instead were obliged to follow only fundamental laws. One then observes the tendency to highlight certain aspects of Jesus' teaching and to ignore others, based on the historical-cultural times. In years past, what was placed in the foreground was undoubtedly the "but I say to you" regarding the indissolubility of matrimony, while at the end of Vatican II, there seemed to be no problem with the theory of a just war. It is undeniable that a shift in thematic emphasis is needed with changing times and the emergence of a culture of non-violence.[32]

But when all is said and done, of what use is the Sermon on the Mount? For a satisfactory answer, perhaps we should primarily consider the *cornerstone* of the sermon. In the opening scene not only are the disciples present, but also the crowd (5:1), which then disappears only to return in the final scene to express their wonder: "And it happened that when Jesus had finished these words the crowds were amazed at his teaching because he was teaching them on his own authority, and not like their scribes" (7:28–29). In this perspective the disciples seem to serve as a bridge. With their testimony they are able to confirm that the Gospel is not only fascinating but also livable. And in this way they are able to help the crowd pass from wonder to following.

However, it is necessary to broaden the idea of who represents the disciples, surmounting the restrictions of an

---

32. I am pleased to remember here the testimony of G. Lanza Del Vasto, founder of the community of l'Arche. He writes these disarming and extremely current words: "Every evil and every injustice begins with error. Who is the evil person? It is a person who is mistaken. This observation is of great importance; it is on this that the foundations of non-violence rest. The first consequence that comes from it is that I find myself exempt from having to hate him. And the second is that I have the elementary and pressing obligation of opening his eyes. The third is that I must knock down, one after the other, his justifications, to the point of standing him alone and naked before his own judgments. The truth will overcome him. I have discovered the solution to conflict" (G. Lanza Del Vasto, *Che cos'è la non violenza.* Milan: Jacabook, 1990; cited by *Avvenire,* November 6, 2001, p. 23).

elect few. The Sermon on the Mount has an inescapable significance for the experience of Christian faith. As John Paul II writes in *Novo Millennio Ineunte*, it proposes "a high standard" of life to which all Christians are called: the way of sanctity in daily life and in ordinary circumstances.

> To ask catechumens: "Do you wish to receive Baptism?" means at the same time to ask them: "Do you wish to become holy?" It means to set before them the radical nature of the Sermon on the Mount: "Be perfect as your heavenly Father is perfect" (Mt 5:48).
>
> As the Council itself explained, this ideal of perfection must not be misunderstood as if it involved some kind of extraordinary existence, possible for only a few "uncommon heroes" of holiness. The ways of holiness are many, according to the vocation of each individual. I thank the Lord that in these years he has enabled me to beatify and canonize a large number of Christians, and among them many lay people who attained holiness in the most ordinary circumstances of life. The time has come to repropose wholeheartedly to everyone this *high standard of ordinary Christian living:* the whole life of the Christian community and of Christian families must lead in this direction (*Novo Millennio Ineunte,* no. 31).

Dialoguing with the Word

- What place does the Sermon on the Mount have in your life? Do you let yourself be guided by the "higher standard" that it proposes?

- The so-called "Golden Rule" was already noted in Judaism, but it was phrased in the negative form:

"Do not do to others..." Jesus formulates it in the positive: *"Do to others what you want them to do to you!"* How do you live this Golden Rule in your family, in your place of work, and in the different relationships that make up your daily life?

CHAPTER FIVE

"He has carried our infirmities"
Descending in order to heal
(Matthew 8–9)

*A*fter having proclaimed the *greater righteousness,* Jesus "descends" the mountain in order to free suffering humanity from evil (8:1). His *descending* (*katabàinô*) recalls the God of the Exodus, who said to Moses: "I have observed the misery of my people who are in Egypt; I have heard their cry on account of their taskmasters. Indeed, I know their sufferings, and I have come down to deliver them" (Ex 3:7–8). God comes down for the sake of the oppressed! The exodus of Israel really begins with the exodus of God, with his descent. He descends to tear his people away from their oppressors, because, as Ephrem the Syrian says so well in a paschal hymn:

> It is hard for the oppressor
> to know that he is an oppressor.
> He does not perceive his own wickedness

as long as he is not oppressed,
until in his oppression he understands
the taste of his own wickedness.[1]

The God of the Bible descends therefore "to tear"[2] Israel out of Pharaoh's fist, and to this end he deploys all his strength in ten prodigies and powerful actions, the so-called "plagues of Egypt." Matthew also lists *ten* prodigies of Christ after he comes down from the mountain. He does not *send plagues,* however, but takes upon himself *our plagues and wounds,* the illnesses and the sorrows of all, as it says in Isaiah 53:4, words strategically placed at the end of the first cycle of miracles: "He took away our illnesses and removed our diseases" (8:17).

This citation offers the hermeneutic key to understanding the profound meaning of Jesus' healing action. The healings spring from his great *compassion.* The Divine Master *comes down* from the mountain to take on the sufferings that oppress humanity, and he calls those who follow him to do the same:

> The Word accomplished his mission by descending, lowering himself to our every darkness, with humility and with a profound love for humanity, for all of us sinners. And so the Church cannot take any other way than that of *kenosis* in order to reveal to the world the Servant of the Lord, the Lamb of God who carries the sins of the world.[3]

---

1. Ephrem the Syrian, *Inni Pasquali* (Milan: Edizioni Paoline, 2001), 128.

2. The Hebrew word *natzàl,* usually translated "to liberate," includes the idea of strength that is better rendered with the verb "to tear away."

3. CEI, *Comunicare il vangelo in un mondo che cambia* (Milan: Edizioni Paoline, 2001), 63.

The ten miracles of the Good Shepherd

Like a good catechist, Matthew regroups, articulates, and inserts material. He employs various techniques to help his readers understand and remember. An attentive glance at the composition of chapters 8 and 9 shows a carefully crafted outline. In the opening verse of chapter 8, the Master is coming down the mountain (8:1); at the end, we see an itinerant Jesus announcing the Gospel and healing the sick, a compassionate shepherd who takes care of his tired and prostrate sheep (9:36–38).

Within this framework three series of miracles are outlined, which bring Christ into direct contact with human marginalization and pain. The third series connects two miracles into one story: the healing of the woman with a hemorrhage and the resurrection of Jairus' daughter. Here follows the outline:

DESCENT FROM THE MOUNTAIN, WITH THE
CROWD FOLLOWING JESUS: **8:1**

First series of miracles (8:2–17)

1. Healing of the leper	8:2–4
2. Healing of the centurion's servant	8:5–13
3. Healing of Peter's mother-in-law and others	8:14–17
Mission and following	8:18–22

Second series of miracles (8:23–9:8)

4. Calming of the storm	8:23–27
5. Liberation of the demoniac	8:28–34
6. Healing of the paralytic	9:1–8
The call of Matthew, the banquet and fasting	9:9–17

Third series of miracles (9:18–34)
7. Healing of the woman with a hemorrhage +
8. resurrection of the daughter of Jairus (one story)   9:18–26
9. Healing of the two blind men   9:27–31
10. Healing of the deaf-mute   9:32–34

    Teaching and healing every disease   9:35

JESUS HAS COMPASSION ON THE CROWDS: **9:36–38**

The three series of miracles are linked by the interconnecting themes of *mission* and *following,* the *call of Matthew* and the festive banquet with the tax collectors. The *concluding summary* is a resumé of the itinerant activities of Jesus, teacher, therapist, and compassionate shepherd.

It is a mosaic of various encounters with people. Spiritual and corporal healings; individuals looking for new paths and meaning; tax collectors whom Jesus approaches and calls to himself; an atmosphere of festivity and freedom, where religious dimensions are rather strict and the space for rigorous observance is narrow. It would be nice to stop over every detail, taking in all the connections and observing the marvelous actions of Christ, but we must content ourselves with looking at just a few points that touch upon the theme we want to deepen: *community and mission.*

The unclean leper, the Gentile, and the woman

The first series of miracles recounts Jesus' solidarity with suffering humanity, in three episodes placed along the road going from the Mount of the Beatitudes to Capernaum. The first episode takes place as soon as Jesus comes down from the mountain; the second, as soon as he enters Capernaum; and the third, as soon as he reaches Peter's house. Within this geographical distance, a far-reaching perspective of salvation unfolds.

Entering progressively onto the scene are *a leprous Israelite*, a *pagan* who intercedes for his servant, and *a feverish woman* who asks for nothing; it is Jesus who takes the initiative and cures her. One immediately intuits that this series of miracles is well aimed and intends to definitively overturn every possible form of marginalization and every cultural and religious barrier.

For our evangelist, Jesus' mission is directed above all to the "lost sheep of the house of Israel" (10:5–6; 15:24); even the miracles correspond to this view. In fact, the first is done in favor of a Hebrew, as can be deduced from the command: "Go show yourself to the priest and present the offering Moses commanded" (8:4). This order would make no sense if it were addressed to a pagan, while it is consistent with what Jesus proclaimed on the mount: that he has not come to *abolish* the Law but to fulfill it. But there is more: the person marginalized because of his impurity is now symbolically sent back beyond the Law, to make a new community that overcomes every barrier between "clean" and "unclean."

Lord, if you wish to, you can make me clean

Unlike Mark and Luke, for whom Jesus' first miracle was an exorcism (Mk 1:23–28; Lk 4:33–37), Matthew opens the series with a leper (8:1–4). Why this deviation? It is not my intention to establish historical truth or determine which evangelist is right. Rather, aware of this diversity of outlook,[4] I would like to understand the reasons supporting Matthew's choice. First of all, why a leper? What does this man's illness represent?[5]

At the time of Jesus, a leper was not merely someone who was sick, but someone who was unclean, condemned because of one's sores to live on the margins of society in the company of people who had lost all hope. At the first symptoms of leprosy (swelling, blotches, exanthema), the afflicted person would have to show him or herself to the priests. If they confirmed the presence of the disease, they would banish the leper from the community to avoid contagion.[6] The leprous person would then have to leave town and live in isolation, crying out to whoever might draw near that he or she was impure. In short, a leper was considered foul, rotting flesh, a kind of walking corpse. To heal someone from leprosy would be like raising that person from the dead. Is this perhaps why Matthew opens the series of miracles with a leper? There are good reasons to support this idea.

---

4. For John, the first miraculous "sign" done by Jesus is the transformation of water into wine at the wedding of Cana: 2:1–11.

5. The healings of the leper and of Peter's mother-in-law is recounted by all three synoptics, while the healing of the Centurion's servant at Capernaum is present in Matthew and Luke but missing in Mark. With slight differences it is also recounted in Jn 4:46–54.

6. In the Bible, leprosy is seen as a punishment. Remember the cases of Miriam, the sister of Moses (Num 12:1–6), and the king, Uzziah, who wanted to offer incense in the temple, abusing his power (2 Chr 26:16–21).

Large crowds followed him when he came down from the mountain and, behold, a leper came up, knelt before him, and said, "Lord, if you wish to, you can make me clean." Jesus reached out his hand, touched him, and said, "I do wish it, be made clean!" and at once his leprosy was made clean. Then Jesus said to him, "See that you tell no one, but go show yourself to the priests and present the offering Moses commanded, as a witness to them" (8:1–4).

Observe the dynamics of this passage. Strangely, this leper does not maintain any distance. He comes right up to Jesus and "kneels before him," as the disciples will later do before the Risen One (28:17: the same verb, *proskynèô*, is used). He calls Jesus "Lord" (*Kyrie*), a title that in the Christian community means precisely the Risen One. Three times the verb *katharìzô*—"to cleanse, to purify"— rings out. The leper's request, highly symbolic, goes beyond physical healing: "Lord, if you wish to, you can make me clean." He is aware that *purification* comes only from Jesus.

And the Lord responds by exceeding the leper's expectations. Jesus is not satisfied with the authoritative word of healing ("I do wish it!"), he adds a concrete gesture. To this fervent leper who has transgressed legal prescriptions to approach him, the Master answers by overcoming the ancient prohibition. Jesus extends his hand and touches him. "I do wish it, be made clean!" Michelangelo's fresco comes to mind; Christ's hand touches the leper as the finger of God touched Adam. The effect is immediate: Jesus heals and purifies, regenerating flesh and spirit.

The story might have ended here, but something else is shown to be important to make sense of this first healing.

The Master follows the miracle with an apparently contradictory command, admonishing the leper not to make known what has happened (Jesus does not look for publicity!), yet sending the man back to competent authorities for the verification of his healing and consequent reentry into the worshiping community. He must keep to the ritual demands prescribed by the Law, consistent with the principle expressed on the mountain: "not to abolish" but "to fulfill" (5:17). In this way the Jewish authorities can have a firsthand experience, a "witness" of Jesus' healing ministry and the healing presence of God among men and women.

But only say the word

The next story (8:5–13) shows a broadening viewpoint; the solidarity of Christ is extended also to the pagans, above and beyond every cultural or religious boundary. This time the important person who asks the favor is a centurion stationed in Capernaum. Centurions were also held to be "unclean," since they were considered the *goyim,* non-Hebrews. But here, surprisingly, it is the pagan who teaches a lesson.

The story can be outlined in four scenes:

— *The encounter* (vv. 5–7). The centurion intercedes for his servant, and the case would seem to end with the Master's prompt response:

> When he entered Capernaum a centurion came up to him, appealing to him and saying, "Lord, my servant is lying paralyzed at home, terribly tormented." Jesus said to him, "I will come and heal him" (8:5–7).

— *The centurion's declaration* (vv. 8–9). Surprisingly, the centurion demonstrates a certain deference, showing that he knows and respects the religious customs of the Hebrew people:

> In response, the centurion said, "Lord, I am not worthy to have you come under my roof—just say a word and my servant will be healed. For I, too, am subject to authority and have soldiers under me, and if I say to this one, 'Go,' he goes, or if I say to another, 'Come,' he comes, and if I tell my slave, 'Do this,' he does it" (8:8–9).

— *Jesus' turning aside to those who have been following him* (vv. 10–12). The scene depicts the Master turning in amazement to those following him: he has not found such faith in Israel!

> When Jesus heard this he was amazed and said to those who were following, "Amen, I say to you, nowhere have I found such faith in Israel! I tell you, many will come from east and west and will recline at table with Abraham and Isaac and Jacob in the kingdom of heaven, but the sons of the kingdom will be thrown out into the outer darkness; there, there will be wailing and gnashing of teeth" (8:10–12).

— *Jesus and the centurion* (v. 13). The Master asserts that this faith will result in a saving effect, and the narrator promptly confirms it by pointing out the miracle:

> Then Jesus said to the centurion, "Go your way! Let it be done for you as you have believed," and the servant was healed at that very moment (8:13).

Let's stop here for awhile. First of all, we might observe the centurion and the sentiments he possesses. Leader of a hundred soldiers, he takes the initiative and asks a favor for a servant who is suffering. A few words reveal that beneath the military uniform this man is remarkably sensitive and profoundly human.

How does Jesus react? In the original text his response can be read two ways. It can have the affirmative sense, as in the proposed translation: "I will come and heal him"; here the Master expresses his willingness to follow the pagan centurion. But another translation is also possible, with the words framed as a question: "Must I come and heal him?" The question would have the purpose of side-stepping the centurion's request based on the awareness previously confirmed in the Gospel of Matthew: Jesus felt that he was sent "only to the lost sheep of the house of Israel" (15:24; cf. 10:7).

Whatever the case may be, the centurion apparently understands the limitations imposed on the Hebrews by the law of purity, and he means to respect it. Besides, he has such faith in Jesus' power that he does not think it necessary to inconvenience the Master. Personal experience has taught him that an order is sufficient to move soldiers and servants. How much more a word from Jesus! How can we not recall the liturgical flavor of these words placed in the mouth of this influential pagan: "Lord, I am not worthy that you should enter my house, but only say the word…"?

The third scene displays an amazed Jesus searching the faces of those following him; he has not found such faith in Israel! And then he looks far away, into the eschatological future where he sees pagans seated at the table in the Kingdom together with Abraham and the other patriarchs of the chosen people. This passage—cited also in Luke 13:28–29, but within another context—takes on a dramatic tone meant to call listeners to conversion. It is not enough to be "natural heirs" of the promises made to Abraham, it is necessary to share his faith. And in this situation, it is the centurion (and those like him) who shows himself to be part of the uninterrupted line descending from the father of believers.

The last scene again focuses in on the two protagonists. Jesus' gaze returns reassuringly to his petitioner: *Let it be done according to your faith!* It is the first healing Jesus performs from a distance. That servant who has been suffering greatly is reached through the centurion's faith. The Gospels record a second case of healing from a distance, which, significantly, involved another pagan: the Canaanite's daughter (15:21–22). "One can see the influx of similar stories that came to the attention of the first Christian missionaries. Like the servant in this account, they too do not encounter Jesus physically; but if they put their faith in him, will not the 'distance' be eliminated and their prayer be heard?"[7]

---

7. Tassin, *Vangelo di Matteo,* 105.

And he touched her hand

The third account (8:14–15) takes place in the house of Peter and immediately focuses on Jesus, who intervenes on his own initiative for the lady of the house, the anonymous mother-in-law of his first disciple:

> And when *Jesus entered* Peter's house *he saw* Peter's mother-in-law **lying** in bed, sick with a fever; *he touched* her hand and the fever left her, and **she got up** and **began to serve him** (8:14–15).

Three verbs describe Jesus' actions: "he entered" (*èlthôn*), "he saw" (*èiden*), and "he touched" (*hèpsato*); and three describe the woman's: "she was lying" (*beblêmènên*), "she got up" (*êgèrthê*), and "she served" (*diêkònei*). Between the actions of the Lord and of the woman there is a space in which the fever must leave, a space of liberty.

In only two short verses the account paints a picture of intense beauty. Guided by a spontaneous movement of his soul, Jesus again stretches out his hand and touches a woman. His hand meets her hand. First he touched the unclean flesh of the leper, and now the feverish hand of the woman.

I like to dwell lovingly on the meeting of those two sets of hands: male and female, like the hands of a bridegroom reaching out to grasp those of his bride. Illness is forced to withdraw. There is no longer space for the oppressive fever; the woman who was lying down is resurrected.

No word emanates from his mouth or from hers. Unlike what happens in the parallel passages from Mark and Luke, in Matthew even those present are silent.

Wrapped in silence, the healing encounter takes place entirely in the interweaving of looks and in that touch of Christ. And immediately the woman "got up" through the energy of his hand. A rising up of body and of soul, a rising up that is *resurrection,* as the verb *êgèrthê,* which later describes the same resurrection of Christ (28:7), suggests.

Set on her feet by the loving glance and healing hand of Jesus, the lady of the house immediately becomes active and oriented; she starts to serve, the *diakonìa.* She is not simply a good servant, but a "deaconess." The last verb that describes her, *diêkònei,* means in fact a ministerial action in the early Church; it is the emergence of the feminine *diakonìa,* service to Christ and to his Word. Not by coincidence does Matthew underline the woman's personal "*diakonìa*" toward Jesus, using the singular "and she served *him*" (8:15), while Mark and Luke use the plural "and she served *them*" (Mk 1:31, Lk 4:39).

In the house of Peter, symbol of the Church, Jesus' hand raises up this woman and makes her a disciple in full liturgical dignity, expressed in the service of love.

And he cured all who were ill

From the parallel passage of Mark we know that the healing of Peter's mother-in-law happened on the Sabbath day (cf. the so-called "day in Capernaum": Mk 1:21–34), a detail that explains why the procession of the sick, which the miracle caused, takes place after sunset (8:16–17). As the Sabbath—and therefore the observance of rest—finishes, people gather before the house where Jesus is a guest. Matthew's account prunes some of the very precise details included in Mark, but adds a personal touch that brings the primacy of the word to the foreground: with nightfall, the Christ whom we have seen touching the leper and taking the hand of the febrile woman now liberates the possessed and cures all sicknesses with simply his word:

> When evening came they brought him many people who were demon-possessed, and he drove the spirits out with a word and cured those who were sick, to fulfill what was said by Isaiah the prophet when he declared, *He took away our illnesses and removed our diseases* (Isa 53:4) (8:16–17).

The series of healings does not end with a festive banquet and intimate joy within Peter's house, but with this river of people pressing around the door, who cause Jesus to come outside. The two paths of our approach to the Gospel of Matthew emerge again, *community* and *mission.*

What strikes me above all is the primary role given to the "word" as an instrument of liberation and healing. I am even more struck because in the parallel passage, Luke highlights the aspect of gesture: "And he laid his hands on each one of them and healed them" (Lk 4:40). The same verb, *etheràpeusen* ("to heal"), is used, but each expresses different ways of healing. Luke emphasizes the gesture, while Matthew stresses the word.

Gesture and word are the great articulations of the sacramental economy. Taking a better look, one discovers an expressive alternation of *gesture* (the hand that touches) and *word* in the sequence of 8:1–17:

> "extending *his hand he touched* the leper";
>   "but only say a WORD...";
> "and *touching her hand*...";
>   "he expelled the spirits with a WORD."

Whether it is the gesture of the hand or the healing word, one notices the liturgical flavor that enfolds Matthew's catechesis. The conclusion seems to say that everything is summarized in the strength of the logo-therapeutic love of Christ.

The second aspect that strikes me is the phrase "all the sick," which seems exaggerated and out of tune in an account meager in comparison to the parallels of Mark and Luke. Matthew thins out Mark's account, which notes that "the whole city was gathered at the door" (Mk 1:33), but Matthew adds an emphatic "all" when it underscores the action of Jesus: "and he cured *all* who were sick." One cannot imagine someone returning home without being healed. Jesus takes onto himself all of our infirmities.

And so we arrive at the third point that I want to emphasize: the fulfillment citation. Our evangelist does not intend to simply recount stories of miraculous healings; above all he wants to demonstrate that in Jesus, God's solidarity with suffering humanity is visible. Jesus personifies the figure of the humble servant of whom the text in Isaiah speaks. He is not afraid of contracting our impurity. The hand that reaches out to touch the wounds of the leper says more about the compassion of God in Jesus Christ than any treatise. He jeopardizes himself for the sake of the outcast and the sick, to the point of bearing our wounds and infirmities. "By his wounds you have been healed," the Apostle Peter will comment, rereading in his turn the prophecy of Isaiah 53 (1 Pt 2:25).

With this first series of healings, Matthew thus anticipates the prospect of the cross, the supreme salvific word of Christ, as though recalling its meaning and soul. Jesus, who heals all the sick and expels demons with his word, is the supreme icon of the passion of God for humanity. Compassion enfolds his entire mission.

Dialoguing with the Word

Enter into personal dialogue with Jesus, who comes down the mountain to heal you too. Try to put yourself into the situations that Matthew describes:

• *The leper* finds the courage to overcome barriers of isolation. He has an immense desire to be healed, and entrusts himself totally to Jesus. Make his invocation your own: *"Lord, if you want to, you can make me clean...."*

• *The centurion* carries the sorrow of another; he prays and intercedes for one of his servants. You, too, can present to the Lord those people who have asked for your prayers. Lay before his healing gaze the sorrowful situations you are aware of. Renew your faith, and make your own the humble invocation: "*Lord, I am not worthy, but only say the word...."*

• *Peter's mother-in-law* asks for nothing; she is simply there, allowing Jesus' loving glance to reach her, letting him take her hand. Allow his gaze to reach your heart and soul, too. Let his hand raise you up and put you back on your feet.

"Courage, my son, your sins are forgiven"

After an initial passage on the following of Jesus, the narration again takes up the Master's missionary activity on the other shore, the eastern side of Lake Tiberius, in pagan territory (8:18). Two fundamental characteristics of his mission are the struggle against evil and the strong appeal of mercy directed to sinners.

The struggle against the forces of evil is illustrated by a new series of miracles, opening with the calming of the storm (8:23–27). The account presents some similarities with the story of Jonah who was sent to the pagans. Notwithstanding the great difference between Jonah, who at first refused to follow God's command, and Jesus, who instead "orders" them to cross to the other side of the lake, like Jonah Jesus sleeps while the storm breaks (cf. Jon 1:5), and, thanks to him, a dead calm ensues, although in a very different way (cf. Jon 1:15). To face the pagan world in order to announce the Kingdom is to walk into a storm, but Jesus takes charge of the sea—which in the Bible is the symbol of evil—and assures those in the boat with him: "Why are you afraid, O you of little faith?" (8:26).

The following miracle takes place directly in the region of the Gadarenes, the name of the people who inhabit that area (ancient manuscripts of the Gospel, however, give it different names: Gerasenes or Gergesenes). There the Master later frees *two* possessed men, described as "coming out of the tombs" (8:28–34). They go to encounter Jesus and immediately, because of the demons that inhabit them, recognize his power and complain that he has come to torment them "before the appointed time." The demons ask for and receive from Jesus permission to enter into a large herd of pigs present in the region, then proceed to throw themselves into the sea, where they perish. For Jews, pigs represent impurity and paganism (cf. 2 Mac 7:1).

Interwoven with various mythical-symbolic elements, the story ends with Jesus being asked to go away; the herdsmen and the entire city are against him! Therefore, the encounter is a failure as regards the mission—and also, it seems, as regards the ones who were cured. What is wrong with them? They remain silent, neither expressing thanks nor taking any kind of responsibility. In the parallel accounts of Mark and Luke (who speak of only one possessed man), Jesus entrusts a mission to the man who was liberated and now asks to follow him: "Go off to your home, to your own people, and proclaim to them everything that the Lord has done for you and how he had mercy on you" (Mk 5:19). Matthew, instead, says nothing. The struggle against evil is not yet won; there is another territory to which Jesus must go. Meanwhile, however, the disciples experience for themselves that where Jesus passes, demons are defeated.

With the healing of the paralytic (9:1–8), the Master and his disciples make their way back to Capernaum, on the western side of the lake, where he shows everyone the face of mercy. The Jesus who returns to "his city" sees beyond appearances, sees the faith of sinners, and turns to the sick with words never heard from anyone before: "Take courage, child, your sins are forgiven" (9:2). *Only someone crazy or blasphemous could make such a claim,* think the scribes who are instructed in the things of God. And they are not mistaken in their point of view.[8] But those who have pondered Matthew's account of Jesus' mysterious origins know that this is precisely the most unique aspect of his mission, in full accord with the information the angel gave about his name: "and you shall call him Jesus, because he will save his people from their sins" (1:21).

Jesus comes down from the mountain and walks along the road of Galilee not only to heal the physically sick, but also and above all those who are spiritually sick. He comes to take away the causes of paralysis and infirmity, to cast out demons, and to liberate from sins. The paralytic is a splendid icon of the mission of Jesus. The Son of Man has the power to give courage to and put a man paralyzed by sins back on his feet again. The vocation of Matthew the tax collector demonstrates this singular aspect of the mission of Jesus, who calls sinners to the banquet table of divine mercy.

Matthew's vocation

Concentrated in a single verse, the call of Matthew nevertheless deserves a profound reading. Others before us have done so—not only exegetes, but artists and painters

---

8. The answer Jesus gives to those who are scandalized by his claims is not a "direct proof," but an argument from the lesser to the greater, where the lesser (making a paralytic walk) transcends the power of men. Both powers instead are attributed to the "Son of Man," to whom God entrusts final judgment (Mt 25:31ff.).

as well—proving that the meager words of the Gospel infuse life, produce creative genius, and inspire art and culture:

> As Jesus traveled on from there he saw a man named Matthew seated at a tax booth, and he said to him, "Follow me." And he got up and followed Jesus (9:9).

Before writing my commentary on this passage, I went again to see Caravaggio's compelling painting, "The Call of St. Matthew," in the Church of San Luigi dei Francesi in Rome. The light bursting forth from the dark scene and illuminating the group of people seated around Matthew does not come from the window, but from the hand of Christ pointing to him. This light coming from Christ's hand depicts the gesture of divine grace and simultaneously asks for a human response. Matthew is hesitant. He almost seems to want to hold onto the money lying on the table, but the left hand of Christ, open and inviting, encourages a prompt response. One has the impression of the divine intersecting with the contemporary. In the painting, only the figures of Christ and Peter are dressed in ancient clothing, while all the others, including Matthew, are dressed in clothes contemporary to the artist. In this way Caravaggio succeeds in expressing with singular realism the attractiveness of the historic present, which Matthew's call encompasses.

Matthew's answer is described with two verbs: "he got up and he followed him." The tax collector's prompt rising from table means the same thing as "leaving everything," which characterized the vocation of the first four disciples

called (4:18–22). Capernaum, a city on the borders, col-
lected ample profits with taxes on the caravans that traveled back and forth from Syria, and taxes from the fishermen of the lake.

The evangelist is sparing with information, but the
thought occurs that the tax collector on whom Jesus
looked must have been unpopular with the inhabitants of
Capernaum and, presumably, also with the four fishermen
whom the Master had already called to himself. *How can
he call this man who takes advantage of us, who gets rich on
collecting taxes on our work?* They are surprised, bewildered.
Not only does Jesus forgive sins, he calls people of ill
repute, sinners, to follow him.

What did the first four disciples think, in their appren-
ticeship of this new profession? "I will make you fishers of
men," Jesus had said (4:19). There is no doubt that here
the Master was catching a "big fish," and that news of
Matthew's conversion would have been the talk of the city.

At the table of sinners:
"It is mercy I desire"

> And it happened that he reclined at table in the house, and,
> behold, many tax collectors and sinners had come and were
> at table with Jesus and his disciples. When the Pharisees
> saw this they said to his disciples, "Why does your teacher
> eat with tax collectors and sinners?" But when Jesus heard
> this he said, "The healthy are not in need of a doctor—the
> sick are. So go learn what this means, *I desire mercy and not
> sacrifice,* for I came not to call the righteous, but sinners"
> (9:10–13).

The scene depicts Jesus at table with the newly-called Matthew, together with "tax collectors and *sinners*," under the indignant gaze of the Pharisees. The phrase "tax collectors and sinners," which sounds familiar to us, reflects the negative judgment circulating at the time for "exactors of taxes." Because of their office, they were people who could easily commit abuses, to such an extent that John the Baptist admonished them, saying: "Collect nothing more than what has been designated for you" (Lk 3:13), while Zacchaeus, "chief tax collector and a rich man," promises Jesus: "Look, Lord, I am giving half of my possessions to the poor, and if I have cheated anyone of anything I am paying it back fourfold" (Lk 19:8).

One therefore understands that Matthew's behavior comes to be openly criticized by the Pharisees, who not incidentally go to the disciples. Perhaps Matthew's conduct stirred up some resentment also in the hearts of James and Peter, two disciples of Jesus particularly attentive to the observance of the Law and religious traditions. One does not picture a rabbi "eating together with tax collectors and sinners," because, as the proverb says: "Tell me with whom you go and I will tell you who you are." A master who was respected must keep the required distance and could not lower himself in such a way.

In the account, the objection is addressed to the disciples, but the response comes from the Master, who in answering saves his companions from embarrassment. He validates his own behavior, basing it on humanitarian and theological reasons. In fact, he has not transgressed but has accomplished the prophetic meaning of the Law. Jesus' response is not given in dogmatic terms; rather it takes the form of a counter-question, which subsequently opens the discussion and makes one think. Who has need of a doctor, the healthy or the sick? Is it not perhaps the duty of a doctor (and should it not be such for a master and shepherd?) to take care of the sick? These questions allow Jesus to reverse the accusation: it is the Pharisees' behavior that is in conflict with the divine plan. Jesus' adversaries consider themselves experts in the Scriptures, but they have not understood a fundamental passage: "It is mercy I want" (Hos 6:6).

The divine will is summarized in mercy. Matthew, who experienced this mercy of God firsthand, cites this passage a second time (cf. 12:7). He is the only author of the New Testament (and also of the first two centuries of Christianity) who cites Hosea 6:6: "It is mercy [*èleos*] I desire and not sacrifice."[9] This strong prophetic text proclaims that true worship pleasing to God is not the offering of animals in the Temple according to the prescriptions of the Law, but the sentiments that inhabit the heart. *Mercy* truly challenges the quality of a person's heart; one could call it the encounter of the *heart* with *mercy*, or rather with the need of the other.

The original *èleos* of the prophet reflects the Hebrew *hèsed*, which primarily means the strong duty, of heart and

---

9. B. Standaert holds that the evangelist of mercy is not Luke, as is usually affirmed, but rather Matthew: "It is mercy I desire," *Parola spirito e vita* 29 (1994/1), 109–119.

action, of the Lord in favor of his people, his choice, and the covenant. But in the Hebrew Scripture the icon of mercy is often depicted in the feminine, since the term that expresses it—*rahamìm*—takes one back etymologically to the maternal bosom (*rèhem*). It brings to mind the womb that carries new life and is full of tenderness for it, and therefore the space made within itself for the life of the other. When it refers to a masculine subject, in particular to a father and to God (it will be said of Jesus further on, in 9:36), it serves to recall that mercy is not simply a question of a body part—the heart, womb, or whatever—but calls into play the will and the whole person.

"It is mercy I want" thus evokes the necessity of opening the heart, and therefore the *house* and the *Church,* not only to those of one's own circle, to the just and the fortunate, but to those who have particular need of kindness and mercy, that is, precisely to the poor and the sick, the sinners and the miserable.

Unfortunately, we note today a "suspicious" attitude with regard to mercy, coming perhaps from Nietzsche's radical criticism of Christianity as "a religion of compassion." At times charity is suspiciously regarded as a way of perpetuating suffering.... But mercy is not commiseration; it is not escaping from oneself to live off of other people's misfortune. It is above all a call to solidarity and to responsibility for the other![10]

---

10. Cf. E. Bianchi, "Peccato e misericordia," *Parola spirito e vita* 29 (1994), 5–6.

Born of divine mercy, the members of the Christian community are called to become in their turn *experts in mercy,* opening their hearts to those who are in suffering.

The compassion of Jesus

The third series of miracles (9:18–33) further illustrates the divine mercy of Christ who cures the sick and raises the dead. The series opens with a double miracle: the healing of the woman with a hemorrhage, who for twelve years had suffered the loss of blood (in the Bible, blood is a symbol of life), and the resurrection of a twelve-year-old girl (9:18–26) who, as the other two synoptics make clear (Mk 5:42; Lk 8:42), was dead. The attentive way in which Jesus turns to the first ("courage, daughter") and the tenderness he shows toward the second ("he grasped the girl's hand and she got up") confirm the words we heard in Matthew's house: "It is mercy I want."

The miracle Jesus works for this woman, so tried in her inmost being that she no longer has any faith in doctors (Mark 5:26 points out that she had spent all she had going from one doctor to another, receiving nothing except humiliation and poverty), could be seen as something "unscheduled," unforeseen by the Master, who instead has in mind to go and heal the young daughter of Jairus.

The woman has been living a devastatingly negative experience, and she approaches Jesus as a last resort for salvation. With all her courage, she gathers the little strength remaining to her and ventures into the sea of people who press her on all sides, making it difficult to breathe. She hopes to be able to reach him at least from behind; it would be enough for her to touch the hem of his garment...

The account that follows these two stories relates the healing of two blind men, who persist in their invocation: "Have mercy [*elèêson*] on us, son of David!" (9:27–31). The two continue their sorrowful pleas as they follow behind Jesus, repeating the word "mercy" (the verb *elèêson* is connected to *èleos*) until they reach the house he has entered. The symbolic aspect of this event can be seen in the fact that it is within the house, the symbol of the Church, that the two men regain their sight. They invoke Jesus as "son of David," a royal messianic title that in the Judaism of Jesus' time carried strong political connotations and the desire for liberation from Roman occupation. Matthew does not refer to this political meaning, however, but connects—both here and in other places—the title "son of David" to the compassion of Jesus and the meekness characterizing his messianic entrance into Jerusalem (cf. the citation of Zech 9:9 in 21:5).

The tenth miracle is an *exorcism* that enables the healed man to speak again: "and when the demon had been driven out the dumb man spoke" (9:33). While Satan gags the man and silences him, Christ gives him back the freedom to speak. This is why others begin to speak and the crowd rejoices: "The like of this has never been seen in Israel!"[11] The *pathos* of God for his people shines in Jesus as it does in no other.

---

11. Naturally not everyone has the same idea. The crowd's enthusiasm is contrasted by the cutting skepticism of the Pharisees, who accuse Jesus of expelling demons with the help of the prince of demons (Mt 9:34).

He went around all the cities and villages

The series of miracles concludes with a medley of the itinerant activity of the Christ (9:35), a summary parallel to 4:23. Jesus' teaching and healings are like two panels that want to be joined together in a profound unity of meaning:

Mt 4:23	*Mt 9:35*
He traveled	Then Jesus
throughout all Galilee,	went around...,
teaching in their synagogues,	teaching in their synagogues,
proclaiming the good news	proclaiming the good news
of the kingdom,	of the kingdom,
and healing every disease	and healing every disease
and illness among the people.	and illness.

But in this passage from Matthew, a kind of bridge also unfolds with a successive discourse on mission. We can look at it in three small units:

— *in the foreground* stands the itinerant mission of Jesus, a pilgrim (*periêgen*) who has as his objective teaching (*didàskôn*), the announcement of the Good News (*kêryssôn*), and the healing (*theapèuôn*) of every infirmity and sickness (9:35);

— *at the center* is the icon of Christ the Good Shepherd, who has compassion on the tired and abandoned crowd (9:36);

— *finally* we are brought back to the disciples and the image of the abundant *harvest* for which *workers* are lacking (9:37–38).

Once more Jesus is depicted in movement, on a journey motivated by a mission that inseparably consists in joyous announcement of the Kingdom and love that cares for and heals. Behold the Good News, the Gospel and its accomplishment in history, in the existential suffering of the poor and the sick to whom Christ went in every city and village. He reveals the merciful love of the Father, making himself a pilgrim and healer in the sanctuaries of human sorrow. The Church must behave no differently, wrote Pope John Paul II. She too is obliged to seek and encounter humanity particularly along the way of its suffering:

> It can be said that man in a special fashion becomes the way for the Church when suffering enters his life. This happens, as we know, at different moments in life, it takes place in different ways, it assumes different dimensions; nevertheless, in whatever form, suffering seems to be, and is, almost *inseparable from man's earthly existence.*
>
> Born of the mystery of the Redemption in the cross of Christ, the Church has to try to meet man in a special way on the path of his suffering. In this meeting man "becomes the way for the Church," and this way is one of the most important ones (*Salvifici Doloris,* no. 3).

He was moved with pity

The image of sheep without a shepherd symbolizes a people left to its own devices, deprived of a capable guide who can guarantee life and security. It is therefore a disoriented and hopeless people.[12] To this people Jesus feels sent:

12. This image is present in the prayer Moses makes to God for his successor. He asks that God choose as leader a man who will precede the peo-

When he saw the crowds he was moved with pity for them
because they were worried and helpless, like sheep without
a shepherd (9:36).

Let us pause over this image of the Shepherd wound-
ed by compassion.[13] The verse begins with the verb *idôn*,
"when he saw." Jesus' gaze stretches profoundly over the
crowd, taking in the uneasiness and suffering that have
moved the people to follow him to seek healing and salvation.

What to others might simply seem like an interesting
or problematic movement of people following a new
prophet, to Jesus instead is a scene that touches the heart
and wounds the soul: "When he saw the crowds he was
moved with pity [*esplanchnìsthê*]." The people stir within
Jesus the divine mercy of God.

This empathetic relating of Christ is well expressed by
the verb *splanchnìzomai*, which, alluding to the "bowels"
(*splànchna*) and in particular to the maternal womb (like
the corresponding Hebrew word, *rahamìm*), evokes a pro-

---

ple so that the community of the Lord will not be "like sheep without a
shepherd" (Num 27:17). The same expression is placed in the mouth of
Micaiah, son of Imlah, when he prophesies the defeat of Israel's troops: "I
saw all Israel scattered on the mountains, like sheep that have no shepherd" (1 Kings 22:17 = 2 Chr 18:16). Judith also makes use of this image
in her discourse to Holofernes: "You will drive them like sheep that have
no shepherd" (Jdt 11:19). The image, therefore, has an ancient flavor; cf.
E. Bosetti, *Il Pastore* (Bologna: EDB, 1990).

13. Beyond my studies on the Shepherd, I suggest the article by F.
Martin, "The Image of Shepherd in the Gospel of Saint Matthew," *Science
et Esprit* 37 (1975), 261–301.

found visceral emotion.[14] Like other Christian writers, Matthew links *splànchna* to *èleos* ("mercy"), a combination that reproposes the Hebraic couplet *hèsed-rahamîm*, which, as we noted earlier, frequently appears in the prophets and psalms.[15] Jesus is the eschatological envoy in whom the mercy of God is made tangible; he is the shepherd full of compassion.

But what does Jesus see in the crowd that so wounds his heart? He perceives a situation of exhaustion and prostration, a kind of utter feebleness. We said that Christ's penetrating gaze could be summed up with the words *eskylmènoi kài errimmènoi*—two verbs that are difficult to understand because they are not found anywhere else in either the New or Old Testament. As for their meaning, they evoke the description the prophet Ezekiel made of the sheep at the mercy of shepherds who were evil and insipid, a metaphor for people who suffer at the hands of their own guides: "My sheep were scattered over all the face of the earth, with no one to search or seek for them" (Ezek 34:6). Since the shepherds do not take care of the

---

14. The verb *splanchnìzomai* recurs five times in Matthew, four of which have Jesus as the subject: 9:36, 14:4, 15:32, 20:34. The other occurrence happens in 18:27, in the context of the parable of the unforgiving servant. Its use is no less significant; in fact, it designates that *kyrios,* "lord," the compassionate one, behind whom it is easy to detect God himself. It is worth noting that in the Greek version of the Old Testament, called the Septuagint, the term *splanchnìzomai* is not used for God, perhaps in order to avoid anthropomorphism, while in the New Testament it is willingly used for Jesus.

15. For example, Isa 63:7; Jer 16:5; Hos 2:21; Ps 25:6, 40:12, 51:3.

sheep but rather of themselves, the flock of the Lord is scattered and abandoned, oppressed, devoured (Ezek 34:10), tyrannized, and afraid (Ezek 34:27–28).

This is a dramatic picture to which Matthew adds a characteristic element: the sheep are seen as "prostrate," exhausted beneath an insupportable weight. In fact, the scribes oppress the people with infinite rules and precepts, placing heavy loads that they will not lift a finger to budge, let alone carry (23:4). Not so Jesus, whose yoke instead is "easy and light" (11:29–30). The duty of a good shepherd is to protect, take care of, bind up, lead back, and give hope (Ezek 34:11–16, 23–31). It is this duty, neglected by the false shepherds but carried out by God, that Jesus incarnates. He makes visible the divine *pathos*. Actually, the Jesus who comes down the mountain and is not afraid of contaminating himself by associating with the unclean and the pagan, who delivers from fever and from demons, who restores hope to the woman, gives sight to the blind, and makes the dumb speak—in short, that varied therapeutic-salvific activity we have titled "the ten miracles of the Good Shepherd"—reveals in an eminent way the *compassion* of God for humanity.

Compassion and prayer

The last two verses switch from a pastoral image to one that is agricultural, from the flock to the golden field of grain—the flock and the laborers of the harvest. Christ's compassion for the crowd cannot be separated from prayer.

> And he said to his disciples, "The harvest is plentiful, but the laborers are few; so implore the Lord of the harvest to send out laborers to his harvest" (9:37–38).

I can picture Jesus traveling through the villages of Galilee, observing fields golden with grain. It is harvest time, but where are the workers? The narrator's attention moves spontaneously from the flock to the field of grain, as if photographing two realities that often co-exist in the countryside of Palestine. But why associate these two images? I think it is because both express the necessity of "someone" who will work, who will take care of. The flock needs a shepherd, the mature harvest needs workers.

What surprises me here is the decidedly unexpected attitude of Jesus. Our spontaneous reaction would be: "Everyone, to work!" Not so Matthew's Jesus, who instead exclaims: "Pray!"

The fields golden with mature grain lead us back to the Lord of the harvest. The disciples are not to jump in hurriedly with automatic initiatives; before all else they must pray for God's intervention, since the mission is his gift. It is not a matter of delaying the mission or in any way dampening one's enthusiasm, but of recognizing the priority of the gift. As they did not become disciples of their own free initiative but because they were called (cf. 4:18–22), so it will be in the vast field of evangelization. This is where Jesus' request for prayer comes from, because God, the unique owner of the flock and the field, will not allow shepherds to be lacking for his flock or workers for his harvest.

Dialoguing with the Word

- Do you feel the compassion of the Good Shepherd for the crowd that is tired and prostrate, for the worried and frenetic people of our time who cannot find meaning or hope? What can you do to be a sign of divine tenderness in the situation in which you live?

- Ask Jesus for his sentiments, that he may convert you to his compassion. Enter into his prayer and invoke the Father to send workers into his harvest.

CHAPTER SIX

"Come to me, all of you"

Attraction and mission

(Matthew 10–12)

*T*he conclusion of Matthew chapter 9 leaves us with the image of an itinerant Jesus. He is completely dedicated to his mission as the Good Shepherd who stoops down to heal sorrow and infirmities. Compassion is the soul of his mission. In Matthew 10 we see how this compassion becomes contagious for the Twelve, whom Jesus called to himself in order to send them to the "lost sheep of the house of Israel" (10:5–6).

Jesus calls others to himself in order to send them out. Because he wants to gather together in unity the dispersed children of God, starting with the lost sheep of Israel, he seeks to draw everyone to himself: "Come to me, all of you" (11:28). Continuing our reading of Matthew, we will stop first at chapter 10, called the "missionary discourse," and

175

then we will look at the two following chapters, which present contrasting reactions to the mission of Jesus, the Master who is humble of heart.

The twelve apostles

Chapter 10 opens with an important scene that sees Jesus at the center of a double movement of attraction and mission. Jesus calls to himself (*pros-kalèô*) in order to send (*apostèllô*). The twelve *disciples* thus become the twelve *apostles.* Here is the first official list of names:

> Then he summoned his twelve disciples and gave them authority over unclean spirits, so they could drive them out and heal every disease and illness. These are the names of the twelve apostles: first Simon who is called Peter and his brother Andrew, and James son of Zebedee and his brother John, Philip and Bartholomew, Thomas and Matthew the tax collector, James son of Alpheus and Thaddeus, Simon the Cananean and Judas Iscariot, who handed him over. Jesus sent these twelve out after instructing them. (10:1–5)

In this passage three verbs describe Jesus' action regarding the Twelve: he "called them to himself" (*proskalesà-menos*); he gave them his power (*èdôken exousìan*) to cast out demons and heal the sick; and finally, he sent them out (*apèsteilen).* This sequence gives us something to think about.

Before conferring the apostolic mandate, Jesus called to himself the twelve disciples, those who were "to follow" the Master unconditionally (cf. 4:18–22; 9:9), as if to confirm their calling, their closeness, their intimate and direct relationship with his person. He who is "close to God" (*pros ton Theòn:* Jn 1:1), or rather "who is in the bosom of the Father" (Jn 1:18) and has heard the beating of this heart of tenderness and compassion, calls disciples to himself, so that before going "to the lost sheep" they would also understand his heart, his sentiments.

In this affective and spiritual closeness a gratuitous gift takes shape, which the disciples receive from all that the Christ himself has received from the Father for the sake of his mission: the power to cast out demons and to cure (*therapèuein*). Jesus makes his disciples participants of his own healing force.

And finally, these twelve (a symbol of Israel and of the Church) are "sent" by him (*apèsteilen*). The very name "apostle" is derived from this verb and means those who are sent, those who are dispatched. It is a sending that reaches disciples of every age and makes the Church a missionary community by its very constitution (cf. 28:18–20).

The missionary discourse

Matthew 10:5–42 gathers together the directives Jesus gives to his Twelve before he sends them on mission, even if, surprisingly, it is not they who leave (as happens in Mk 6:12 and Lk 9:6), but Jesus himself: "And it happened that when Jesus had finished instructing his twelve disciples he left there to teach and preach in their cities" (11:1).

Jesus' mission creates the frame or setting for the whole discourse. In fact, 11:1 recalls the summary of chapter 9:

Framework:

> Then JESUS went around all the cities and villages, *teaching in their synagogues and preaching....* (9:35)

DISCOURSE ON MISSION (Mt 10:5–42)

Framework:

> And it happened that when JESUS had finished instructing his twelve disciples *he left there to teach and preach in their cities* (11:1).

If we look at the complex structure of the discourse, what emerges is a concentric set-up that revolves around the principle of conformity: as the Master, so the disciple; as the Christ, so the Church.

a) Instruction to the ones sent: gratuitousness and welcome (10:5–15)

> b) *Announcement of persecutions* (10:16–23)
>
> **c) As the Master, so the disciples (10:24–25)**
>
> bb) *Confidence during persecutions* (10:26–39)

aa) Instruction to the ones sent: welcome (10:40–42)

The first and last citations have the theme of welcome in common, the middle texts (b and bb) give advance notice of sufferings and persecutions, while the central passage (c) develops the principle of the disciple's conformity with the Master.

The tone of the whole chapter is decidedly missionary. One has the distinct impression that the Lord (and the evangelist) wants to put this group in motion, as if releasing it from a position of immobility. This is a group without any other ties, completely dedicated to the task received. There is the need "to go," to break through resistances and extend the mission of Jesus—with uncalculated courage and complete confidence in the one primarily interested in the successful outcome of the "mission."

It is a program permeated with the spirit of the Gospel, a style that closely follows that of Jesus, a horizon that goes beyond the historical activity of the Twelve and outlines the missionary statute for the disciple of every age.

A priority: the lost sheep of Israel

But the exhortation Jesus delivers in the discourse sounds surprisingly restrictive: "Do not go off on the road to the Gentiles, and do not enter a Samaritan city; go, instead, to the lost sheep of the house of Israel" (10:5–6). Why this imposed limitation, which seems to contradict the openness suggested in the preceding section with the episode of the centurion and the one that took place in pagan territory (8:28–34)? Evidently this means that the mission field is not yet universal.

We find the phrase again in 15:24, where Jesus responds this way to the disciples who ask him to listen to the Canaanite woman: "I have only been sent to the lost sheep of the house of Israel." Matthew could not have invented these words. So how do we interpret this directive, which seems to limit the missionary prospects of his Gospel?

According to some Scripture scholars, there is an evolution in Jesus' missionary consciousness, which progressively broadens to the point of maximum universal openness, in line with the solemn poems of the Servant of the Lord. "It is too light a thing that you would be my servant to raise up the tribes of Jacob and to restore the survivors of Israel; I will give you as a light to the nations, that my salvation may reach to the end of the earth" (Isa 49:6). In Isaiah, therefore, the prospect is definitely universal, but coming from that sign which is the restoration of Israel.

Adopting a similar historical-theological perspective, Matthew shows that Jesus was faithful to his own mission as Messiah of Israel. He entered into partnership with the Twelve, an eloquent symbolic number since it recalls the twelve tribes, that is, all of Israel unified. Perhaps in the early Church there still might have been Christians coming from Judaism, or Judeo-Christians, who opposed the mission to the Gentiles, justifying their position with the very words of Jesus. The evangelist does not deny this, but he assumes it in a perspective that goes from the particular to the universal, from Israel to people of all nations. In the end, the Risen One clearly reinforces this perspective:

"All authority in heaven and on earth has been given to me. Go, therefore, and make disciples of all nations, baptizing them in the name of the Father and of the Son and of the Holy Spirit, and teach them to observe all that I have commanded you and, behold, I will be with you all the days until the end of the age" (28:18–20).

Therefore, a mission first of all to "the lost sheep of Israel." In this way Matthew also shows that Jesus has fulfilled the promises of the Old Testament—in the present situation, by gathering the dispersed Israel:

"I myself will be the shepherd of my sheep, and I will make them lie down, says the LORD God. I will seek the lost, and I will bring back the strayed, and I will bind up the injured, and I will strengthen the weak, but the fat and the strong I will destroy. I will feed them with justice" (Ezek 34:15–16).

There is thus a progression in Christ's mission, and this aspect also teaches the Church, whether in regard to Judaism or to the internal behavior of the community. There is need to begin with the "ones far away" who are closer, as Jesus began, so to speak, with those of his own house. "Being far away" does not only mean in a spatial sense; it is a way of being. One can be far away even though living within the same walls.

Christ's compassion extends itself in the first place to his own people. On one hand, this fact sharpens the drama of Israel, which does not recognize its own Messiah. The evangelist John will say: "He came to his own home, yet his own people did not receive him" (Jn 1:11). But this does not remove the *priority* of the mission to Israel. Even Paul respected this in his missionary journeys, offering the Gospel first of all to the Jews of the Diaspora, and then to the Gentiles (cf. Acts 13:5, 14, 46–48).

And as you go, proclaim

"As you go, proclaim the good news, and say, 'The kingdom of heaven is at hand.' Heal the sick, raise the dead, cleanse lepers, drive out demons" (10:7–8).

Missionaries of the Gospel must first awaken hope: *Raise your head and see, God is doing something new, his Reign is coming!* The saving proximity of the Reign, which

constitutes the joyful announcement, must make itself
known with signs: "heal the sick, raise the dead, cleanse
lepers, drive out demons...." Jesus inaugurates a mission of
hope, an invitation to grasp the signs of divine mercy, a
breath of fresh air for exhausted and prostrate sheep.

The disciples were sent to accomplish the same *signs*
worked by the Master, narrated in chapters 8 and 9, *signs*
pointed out to the Baptist as proof of the Messiah (11:4–5).
Like the apostles, Christians of every time are called to
be heralds of the joyful news that releases liberation and salvation; they are called to proclaim a love that saves, heals,
and generates life.

Freely you have received, freely give

The activity and behavior of those who are sent must
be permeated with that gratuitousness they have experienced in their relationship with the Lord: *dôreàn elàbete,
dôreàn dòte*, "Freely you have received, freely give" (10:8).
Only Matthew transmits this saying of the Master—four
words in all, with two verbs preceded by the same adverb
marking the rhythm of the passage. It is a term that refers
to the "gift."[1] Jesus has lived the spirituality of the gift:
"Everything has been given to me by my Father," he will
say enthusiastically in his hymn of praise (11:27). And it
will later be confirmed by the Risen One: "All authority in
heaven and on earth *has been given to me*" (28:18)

---

1. *Dôreàn* occurs only here in Matthew and eight times in the entire
New Testament: see Rom 3:24; 2 Cor 11:7; Rev 21:6.

The disciples are now associated with a dimension of gratuitousness like the breath of the spirit of the Gospel. And what have they received gratuitously? The context points out three fundamental aspects: the call of Jesus; participation in his power, which enables the disciples to expel demons and cure every sickness and disease; and finally the same announcement, the Good News of the Kingdom.

Aren't these gifts for us, too? Have we paid to receive life, the Gospel, freedom from our sins, or the divine adoption? Then let the song resound that should give rhythm to the steps of the Church in mission: *freely you have received, freely give.* It is a double movement of the heart, to receive and to give, in full harmony with the gift.

Do not keep gold or silver; neither a bag for the road nor two tunics!

Gratuitousness accompanies a style of poverty that must witness to the full confidence of the ones sent in the One who is at the source of the mission: the Lord of the harvest! "Do not keep gold or silver," says Matthew, who unlike Mark and Luke does not forbid carrying money, but *accumulating* it. Once more, gratuitousness appears in the foreground. Each Gospel adapts the Master's directives to concrete situations. For Matthew this means no change of clothes, no sandals, not even a stick for the journey, which could serve not only as a support, but also as a defensive weapon. The one being sent must present himself without defenses, trusting totally in his Lord. Lack of provisions—even of a knapsack—illustrates complete confidence.

I would like to share a reflection here that might make you laugh, but I believe it will help in understanding the original depth of this directive regarding clothing, which to me connects directly with the way Jesus lived. How could the Master require his disciples not to have "two tunics" if he himself had a change of clothes? And realistically, if we imagine Jesus with only one tunic (the one without a seam, sewn all in one piece from top to bottom, which was not divided among the soldiers but for which they cast lots; cf. Jn 19:23–24), then our way of picturing the Master has to change a bit.

Usually, prompted by iconographic art, we imagine him in a clean and washed tunic. But if Jesus walked the sunny roads without a change of clothes, what he wore had to smell rather of dust and sweat.... In short, without including him in the category of the wretched (for whom it would be a luxury even to own one tunic!), what emerges from this passage is an earthy Jesus.

The logic behind this extremely radical style is the same as that of the Sermon on the Mount: Have complete confidence in the one sending you, the Lord of the harvest. If the birds of heaven do not sow or reap and the Father feeds them, how much more should the ones whom he sends not carry a knapsack in order to have bread![2] On the other hand, those sent are not mendicants but "work-

---

2. The comparison with the birds returns expressly in 10:29–31, to support the reason for one's confidence: "Are not two sparrows sold for a few cents? Yet not one of them will fall to the earth without your Father's leave.... So do not be afraid; you are worth more than many sparrows!"

ers" (9:37–38), and as such have a right to their own sustenance. Therefore they will accept willingly the welcome given to them. The Father's providential care will be concretely demonstrated in hospitable houses from which the Gospel can irradiate to the whole city, as it was for Jesus in the houses of Peter at Capernaum and Martha in Bethany (cf. Lk 10:38). Entering such a house, the apostle will say *Shalom*, a peace that has the ring of Christ to it.

Like sheep in the midst of wolves

> "Behold, I am sending you off like sheep among wolves; be as wise as serpents and guileless as doves. But beware of men. They will hand you over to councils, and scourge you in their synagogues, and you will be led before governors and kings for my sake, as a witness to them and to the Gentiles. But when they hand you over, do not worry about how you are to speak or what you should say; for what you should say will be given to you in that hour, for it will not be you speaking but the Spirit of my Father speaking in you" (10:16–20).

Jesus does not promise his apostles an easy life, but rather his same destiny marked by adversity and persecutions. He is aware of the violence that inhabits the world, of the abuse of power wielded by the strong over the weak, of the fact that man is often a *wolf* among his fellows. But Jesus' logic is diametrically opposed to such behavior. He presents himself as a *lamb*, in complete meekness and without violence, along the lines of the prophet Jeremiah (Jer 11:19) and the anonymous Servant of the Lord (Isa 53:6–7; cf. Acts 8:26–35). Jesus recognizes himself *in the poor of YHWH,* those meek and humble persons for whom he is their interpreter and greatest advocate: "Learn from me, for I am gentle and humble hearted" (11:29). And in turn he sends the disciples "as lambs in the midst of wolves."

The metaphor Jesus uses does not have an exact parallel in the Bible, but expresses well the spirit of many of its pages and in particular of certain psalms.[3]

From this passage and from the teaching of Jesus there emerges the strong conviction that the meek, although they lose on the historical level, will reveal themselves victorious in the lasting future of God. In the end, the wolf will live with the lamb, the panther with the goat, the calf with the lion (Isa 11:6–7). We are sent in the midst of wolves with the confidence that, in the end, meekness will win. The blood of the martyrs, of many innocent lambs sent to the sword, will not remain silent, buried by history. It becomes good seed for the coming future of God, in whom the meek will inherit the earth (Mt 5:5).

Prudent as serpents, simple as doves

To face the hostile world, Jesus proposes two apparently contradictory but necessary virtues: prudent shrewdness and candid simplicity.

---

3. A story is told of a dialogue that took place between the Emperor Hadrian and Rabbi Jehoshua, in which the emperor says to the rabbi: "Great is the sheep that can resist seventy wolves," alluding to Israel in the midst of pagans. And the rabbi answers: "Great is the shepherd who frees [the sheep] and cares for it and smashes them before it" (*Midrash Tanhuma,* Parashat Toledot, 5).

Shrewdness is not only the ability to deceive, as the serpent did in Genesis 3; it is also the ability to discover deception in order to escape it. And simplicity is not the carelessness of one who steps into peril, but rather the confidence of a baby in its mother. Those who are sent must therefore have the prudence not to expose themselves to evil and the confidence to win in spite of it. "The first [task] is to avoid danger when it is possible; the second is to confront it when it is unavoidable."[4]

The rest of the discourse (10:17–25) can be read as a practical application of this combination of prudence and simplicity. Prudence is appreciating reality and recognizing that hostility and persecutions will occur. Like Jesus, the disciples will be handed over to tribunals and scourged (cf. 2 Cor 11:23ff.; Acts 5:40; 6:12; 22:19). *"Flee!"* To possess the shrewdness of a serpent means to have the intelligence not to expose oneself to evil. Jesus himself "escaped" as often as he could, for example when the Pharisees decided that he must perish for having healed a man on the Sabbath: "Now Jesus realized this and departed [*anechôresen*] from there" (12:15). It is a strategic withdrawal, an escape that enables him to continue his mission until he reaches the hour determined by the Father, when he will no longer be able to escape (26:50). But until that hour, there is room for prudent shrewdness, which succeeds in withdrawing or avoiding places of power. Jesus

---

4. S. Fausti, *Una comunità legge il Vangelo di Matteo*, 2 vols. (Bologna: EDB, 1998), I, 185–186.

does not teach us to run into the arms of martyrdom, because the Christian martyr is not one who seeks death but who wants life and love, whatever the price he or she must pay.

It is enough for the disciple to become like the master

We are at the central point or keystone of the discourse, seen even from a structural point of view:

> "The disciple is not above the teacher, nor the servant above his master. It is enough for the disciple to become like his teacher, and the servant like his master. If they have called the householder Beelzebul, all the more will they revile his dependents!" (10:24–25)

These two verses express the principle of conformity: as the master, so the disciple. Undoubtedly this reflects a privileged relationship of intimacy: it is to be in perfect communion of life and destiny with that Master and Lord who healed the sick and expelled demons in spite of those who accused him of silencing them through the prince of demons (9:34; 12:24). How then can the disciple expect recognition and success in the mission when his Master was blamed and contradicted? On the contrary, if the disciple too experiences opposition and adversity, it is a sign that he or she is on the right road and is following Jesus. The disciple's honor lies in sharing life and destiny with the Lord (*kyrios*) and Master (*didàskalos*).

> ### *Dialoguing with the Word*
>
> • Reflect on the meekness inherent in the phrase: "as
>   lambs in the midst of wolves." How does one live
>   this meekness in the political sphere, or in the midst
>   of fierce economic and social competition?
>
> • Compare yourself with Jesus, the lamb whom the
>   Father sent in the midst of wolves. What does it
>   mean for you today, in your concrete reality, to be a
>   disciple of the Master who is meek and humble of
>   heart?

A mission that is opposed

> And it happened that when Jesus had finished instructing
> his twelve disciples he left there to teach and preach in their
> cities. (11:1)

For Matthew, Jesus remains the great protagonist of
mission; it is he who leaves in order to preach. The disciples are still in the phase of learning the gratuitousness and
dedication of Jesus by following him. They are also learning from him the occasions in which to adopt the prudent
shrewdness of the serpent and the simplicity of the dove.

Before the discourse on mission, the evangelist had
pointed out contrasting reactions Jesus encountered: enthusiastic on the part of the people, unfavorable on the
part of the Pharisees (9:33–34). Now, however, opposition
tightens around him to the point of causing the Master to
prudently retreat; it is a distancing, if not a real escape.

But the Pharisees went out and plotted to do away with
Jesus. Now Jesus realized this and departed from there
(12:14–15).

The account unfolds in a dramatic crescendo that goes
from the doubt gripping the Baptist to the indifference of
many (11:2–19). Not even the lake cities, witnesses of
great miracles, are converted. But notwithstanding the
strong reproof Jesus gives them for this (11:20–24), he
unexpectedly breaks into a hymn of praise (11:25–30). He
knows how to recognize the Father's action, which surprisingly hides the mystery from the wise and reveals it to
little ones, inviting all to share his destiny.

"Are you he who is to come?"

A question haunts the Baptist from the dungeon where
Herod holds him prisoner. That question has to do with
Jesus as Messiah. "The one coming after me is more powerful than I am," the Baptist had said to his disciples on the
banks of the Jordan. He imagined the Messiah differently,
with the winnowing fork in his hand to separate good grain
from the chaff. He thought Jesus would fulfill the divine
judgment, thus answering the immense thirst for justice
that covered the earth. But so far this had not happened.
Had he been mistaken? In the solitude of his prison a terrible doubt assails John. And I imagine that this doubt of
having been mistaken in his messianic expectation did him
more harm than those keeping him prisoner.

John, however, does not give in to cynicism. Rather
than drawing the conclusion himself and dismissing the

Awaited One since he does not correspond to John's expectation, he proposes the question directly to Jesus: "Are you he who is to come, or are we to expect another?" (11:3). I picture him even gaunter than when he was in the desert calling people to repentance. Now John is pure invocation.

How does Jesus answer him? Not in a way that would satisfy our demand for clarity, with a typical yes or no. The Master allows the facts, the signs of mercy, to speak for him:

> "Go tell John what you hear and see: The blind can see again and the lame walk, lepers are made clean and the deaf hear, the dead are raised and the poor are given the good news; and blessed is whoever is not scandalized by me" (11:4–6).

Jesus lists six prodigies in favor of the blind, the lame, the leper, the deaf, the dead, and the poor. In other words, he sends word to his precursor: You are not mistaken in the One you expected; in fact, the signs of the Messiah are accomplished as they were announced by the prophets (cf. Isa 35:5–6 and 61:1); but you are mistaken in the way in which you understand his coming. You expected a Messiah who would judge, but God decided to visit the earth with overwhelming mercy. Rather than judgment first and then salvation, the Reign of God that moves forward with me is about the contrary. Do not be scandalized, John, by the about-face!

The conclusive beatitude, "and blessed is whoever is not scandalized by me," is certainly directed to the Baptist, but reaches believers of every time with their own doubts.

Naughty children who spoil the game

After the conversation with the Baptist's messengers, Jesus criticizes his listeners' behavior, comparing them to capricious children who do not know how to play the game. This game to which the Master refers has two sides. Who knows how many times he saw it played in the marketplaces of the villages of Galilee; how many times he too played it as a child? As is well known, children live for imitation, and two events were usually mimicked: dances at a wedding feast and lamentations for mourning. When the flute was played, one had to dance for the wedding feast, and when the lament was intoned, one had to imitate the mourners. But here we have capricious and argumentative children, who refuse to dance or lament, irritating their friends and ruining the game:

> "But to what shall I compare this generation? It is like children sitting in the marketplace who call to each other and say, 'We piped for you and you did not dance, we wailed for you and you did not mourn.' For John came neither eating nor drinking, and they said, 'He has a demon'; the Son of Man came eating and drinking, and they said, 'Look at him, a glutton and a drunkard, a friend of tax collectors and sinners.' Yet wisdom is justified by her works" (11:16–19).

Jesus compares his contemporaries to spiteful children who do not play along with God (who seriously plays within history). They have eluded both John's call to repentance as well as the joyous message of Jesus, accusing him of being a party person, "a glutton and a drunkard, a friend of tax collectors and sinners." The judgment, anything but kind, which these contemporaries express about the Baptist and the Nazarene, is commented on as being foolishness and an inability to play along with God; to understand the right time. They do not respect his freedom to speak and to intervene through a style that is apparently contradictory. In fact, one who is wise understands that his constant project of love calls always and in different ways to conversion.[5]

At this point of the story, Matthew's Jesus expresses first lament (11:20–24) and then praise (11:25–27). Here first is the lament:

> Then he began to denounce the cities in which most of his mighty works had taken place, because they had not repented. "Woe to you, Chorazin! Woe to you, Bethsaida! Because if the mighty works that happened in you had taken place in Tyre or Sidon, they would have repented in sackcloth and ashes long ago. But I say to you, it will be more tolerable for Tyre and Sidon on the day of judgment than for you. And you, Capernaum! You will be exalted to heaven, will you? You will be brought down to hell! Because if the mighty works that happened in you had taken place in Sodom it would have remained to this day. But I say to you, it will be more tolerable for the land of Sodom on the day of judgment than for you!" (11:20–24)

Chorazin, Bethsaida, and Capernaum are the cities that most greatly benefited from Jesus' presence, from his preaching and pastoral healing. The Master had expected

---

5. Cf. E. Bosetti and A. Niccacci, "The demon-possessed and the party person. Lk 7:34–35 (Mt 11:18–19), based on the biblical-Judaic wisdom tradition," in *Early Christianity in Context: Monuments and Documents,* edited by F. Manns and E. Alliata (Jerusalem: Franciscan Printing Press, 1993), 381–394.

a response of conversion that was never forthcoming. And what follows next? I am very much impressed that Matthew places praise after this lament. The Master is not stopped when faced with a meager apostolic balance sheet. The prophetic "woe" against the impenitent cities gives way to a hymn of praise. Jesus seems to interpret precisely the two opposite sides of God's "game," which are revealed in history: frustration and joy, complaint and praise.

The passage of Matthew 11:25–27 is transmitted in an almost identical form in Luke. Here is the synopsis:

Lk 10:21–22	*Mt 11:25–27*
"I praise you, Father,	"I praise you, Father,
Lord of heaven and earth,	Lord of heaven and earth,
because you hid these things	because you hid these things
from the wise and intelligent	from the wise and intelligent,
and revealed them to babes;	and revealed them to babes;
yes, Father, for such	yes, Father, for such
was your desire.	was your desire.
All things have been	All things have been
given to me	given to me
by my Father,	by my Father,
and no one knows	and no one knows
who the Son is	the Son
except the Father,	except the Father,
nor who the Father is	nor does anyone know the Father
except the Son,	except the Son,
and whoever the Son	and whoever the Son
chooses to reveal him to."	chooses to reveal him to."

Jesus expresses himself in a moment of jubilation, vibrant with praise and wonder. He exalts the Father, creator of the universe, because he acts in a completely surprising way, hiding from the wise and revealing to children. This *hiding and revealing* is part of the obliging game of God. So it pleases the *Father* (a term that recurs with expressive frequency in this verse—a good five times!).

Here Jesus publicly recognizes the Father's revealing action, and he does so with a joyous face, expressing profound emotion. He has understood the Father's secret and his surprising action, which turns human schemes upside down.

The Son bears witness to full reciprocity with the Father, a perfect correspondence of love. He claims the exclusiveness of that relationship, affirming that no one knows the Father if not his Son. But he immediately adds that he has the power to introduce whomever he wishes into this filial relationship (11:27). These verses are justly held among the highest words of the synoptic Gospels, close through mystical inspiration to the discourse of the Last Supper in the Gospel of John (14–16).

One can also see here a kind of attraction for mission. In effect, the divine, "substantial" attraction, which unites the Father to the Son and the Son to the Father, does not exhaust itself in mutually intimate relationship. This loving intimacy opens itself to universal welcome, since the Son can introduce whom he wants into his rejoicing, into the dance of the sons.

Come to me, all of you!

> "Come to me, all you grown weary and burdened, and I will
> refresh you. Take my yoke upon you and learn from me, for
> I am gentle and humble hearted, and you will find rest for
> your souls; for my yoke is easy, and my burden light"
> (11:28–30).

Only Matthew records these words in close proximity
to Jesus' cry of exaltation and intimacy with the Father.
There is no doubt that at an editorial level they constitute
the logical conclusion to the preceding passage, a conclusion even more revealing in what it lacks in the parallel
passage from Luke.[6]

Matthew's inclusion and adaptation of this *logion* (saying of Jesus) has a pastoral aim. It deals with the invitation
to an intense following as disciples. One must learn from
Jesus, who is meek and humble of heart, agreeing to carry
his "yoke." The attention is on Jesus inasmuch as he is the
giver of a new discipline ("yoke") of obedience. But if one
does not want to reduce the importance of 11:28–30 to
moralism, one must consider the connection with the preceding passage, with the revelation of the Father to the little ones and with that unique knowledge of love that
unites the Father to the Son and vice-versa.

---

6. It is surprising that this conclusion is missing in Luke. These verses
are probably not part of the so-called "Q source" (the ancient collection of
sayings and facts about Jesus common to Matthew and Luke) from which
Mt 11:25–27 = Lk 10:21–22 is taken. Otherwise, one would not understand why Luke had omitted such a significant saying of the Master,
which, among other things, agrees with the preference Luke fosters for
the humble and the oppressed.

Therefore, the invitation "come to me, all of you"[7] concludes a hymn of praise and blessing that we can call the "*Magnificat* of Jesus" (11:25–27). He cannot contain his wonder and joy in contemplating the "subversive" action of the Father who, contrary to expectations, reveals his mystery to the little ones. Jesus invites us to enter into his joy in full knowledge of the gift. His attitude diametrically opposes that of Adam, who in the Garden of Eden was suspicious of God and stole the forbidden fruit. "Everything has been given to me," sings instead this joyous Son of the Father, who receives everything as a gift of his love.

Three imperatives and other promises

Let us stop for a moment to consider the structure of Matthew 11:28–30. Three imperatives emerge, accompanied by a promise and/or a motivation:

Imperatives	*Promises (P)/Motivations (M)*
1. Come after me	I will give you rest (P)
2. Take my yoke upon you	for my yoke is easy and light (M)
3. Learn from me	because I am meek and humble (M)
	and you will find rest (P)

---

7. Such an invitation is fundamental to the charismatic experience of Blessed James Alberione, founder of the Pauline Family, who wrote: "The night that divided the last century from the present one [1900–1901] was decisive for the specific mission and particular spirit in which his future mission was to be born and live. After the solemn midnight Mass in the cathedral [of Alba], the Blessed Sacrament was exposed for adoration.... A special light came from the Host, a greater understanding of the invitation extended by Jesus: 'Come to me, all of you....'" (G. Alberione, *Abundantes divitiae gratiae suae,* edited by A. Colocrai and E. Sgarbossa. Rome: Edizione Paoline, 1998, 13–14).

As you might notice, the third imperative is followed by a motivation *and* a promise. The reason for both is not revealed immediately but at the end of the passage to which it is linguistically connected. The entire text, symmetrically arranged, is centered on a statement made only once:

a) COME to me, all you who are weary and BURDENED
    b) and I will give you *rest*.
        c) TAKE *my yoke* upon you
            d) and LEARN from me, for I am meek and
                humble of heart
        bb) and you will find *rest* for your souls
    cc) for *my yoke* is easy
aa) and my BURDEN is light.

The structure of this small literary unit places the third imperative and its motivation at the center: "Learn from me, because I am meek and humble of heart." And this underscores the theme's relevance.

The master of the meek heart

There is a strong resemblance between Jesus' invitation and that extended by the personification of Wisdom, who in Sirach 51 says:

> Draw near to me, you who are uneducated,
> and lodge in the house of instruction.
> Why do you say you are lacking in these things,
> and why do you endure such great thirst?
> I opened my mouth and said,
> Acquire wisdom for yourselves without money.
> Put your neck under her yoke,

and let your souls receive instruction;
it is to be found close by.
See with your own eyes that I have labored but little
and found for myself much serenity (Sir 51:23–27).

The similarity between the words of Jesus and those of Ben Sirach center around three terms in particular: to work hard (*kopiàô*), to find rest (*heurìskô, anàpausis*), and yoke (*zygos*). Other similar texts come from Wisdom readings, particularly Sirach 6:19, 28–30, 24:18–21, and 51:23–27; but also Proverbs 1:20–33 and 8:1–36; and Jeremiah 6:16. Here as on many other occasions the Teacher of Nazareth aligns himself with the ancient teachers of Israel, to whom he is indebted for this Wisdom literature.[8]

Ben Sirach speaks of the yoke of wisdom, while Jesus speaks of his own yoke and of the necessity of learning from him. At first glance this can seem a juxtaposition.[9] It is not, however, for Jesus is not opposed to the wisdom-law but to the way of interpreting it. He is not opposed to the Torah (the Law or the Pentateuch) insofar as it is the

---

8. There are those who hold that Mt 11:28–30 might be a citation from a Hebrew wisdom book, but others do not know or see the need for it. As Manson rightly observes: "If the author of Ecclesiasticus can think in such words, so can Jesus": T. W. Manson, *I detti di Gesù nei Vangeli di Matteo e di Luca* (Brescia: Paideia, 1980), 296. See further: F. Christ, *Jesus Sophia: Die Sophia-Christologie bei den Synoptikern* (Zürich: Zwingli, 1970), 110–119; M. J. Suggs, *Wisdom, Christology, and Law in Matthew's Gospel* (Cambridge, MA: Harvard University Press, 1970), 77ff.

9. This is what Manson, Hunter, and Martin mean when they speak of the yoke of Jesus being contrasted with that of the Law; M. Maher differs: "Take my yoke upon you" (Mt 11:29)," *New Testament Studies* 22 (1976), 97–103, and C. Deutsch, *Hidden Wisdom and the Easy Yoke. Wisdom, Torah, and Discipleship in Matthew 11:25–30* (Sheffield: JSOT, 1987).

revealed Word, but rather to the *halakàh*, that is, to the
directives of the rabbis—specifically of the "scribes and
Pharisees," who determined the behavior of the people
down to the minutest detail, imposing on them an insupportable weight (Mt 23:4).

Jesus does not set himself up against the Law as such;
neither is his yoke opposed to that of wisdom. His is the
yoke of the Reign. Therefore he fully recognizes the sov-
ereignty of God and requires unconditional obedience to
his plan, as the Law received on Sinai already asked for.[10]
But Jesus leads us back to the Law, and therefore to the old
revelation and its original function, which is that of safe-
guarding human persons and not oppressing them beneath
overwhelming religious burdens.

The comparison then is between the pharisaic interpretation of the Law, which oppresses, and that of Jesus
expressed in the mercy of God, author of the very same
Law. The scribes imposed heavy loads on others (cf. Mt
23:4); Jesus gives rest to the weary and the oppressed, first
of all by revealing his filial relationship with the Father.
Jesus' yoke is not taken up merely in theory, but in learning
his attitudes, in sharing his way of thinking and living. All
who are oppressed are invited to come to him to find "rest."

---

10. Indirectly the evangelist introduces a veiled polemic against a certain libertinism that rejected the ethical requests of the Gospel. In this
sense, the saying of R. Nehunya b. Ha-Kanah (circa A.D. 70) could be
applied also to the words of Jesus: "The one who takes upon himself the
yoke of the law will be liberated from the yoke of the kingdom (that is,
from the oppression of the powerful of this world) and from the yoke of
worldly cares" (Abot 3:5).

Rest (*menuhàh*) is a common idea in Wisdom and Deuteronomist tradition; it includes the enjoyment of peace (*shalòm*), the sum of all goods. The expression evokes the rest prepared for the disciple of wisdom (Sir 51:27), the rest of the pious Israelite in the land given by the Lord (Deut 12:9; Jer 6:16), the restful waters of Psalm 23: "The LORD is my shepherd...he leads me beside still waters."

"Learn of me," says Jesus, "who am *meek and humble of heart.*" The expression describes his identity, his heart (*kardia*) and his way of living.

Let's explore the meaning of this central phrase. The adjectives *praos* and *tapeinòs,* usually translated as "meek and humble," are rather rare terms in the Gospels. *Praos* appears three times, and only in Matthew (5:5, 11:29, and 21:5, where the citation refers to the prophet Zechariah); the only other place the word appears is in First Peter 3:4. We find *tapeinòs* twice in the Gospels: once in Matthew 11:29 and the other time in Luke 1:52 (it recurs six times in the rest of the New Testament; the verb, however, is used more frequently). The two adjectives appear together only here to indicate the humility of Jesus, that humility of heart (*tês kardiàs*) which in the Bible characterizes the attitude of the "poor of the Lord." In fact, in the linguistic use of the Septuagint, above all in the psalms, *praos* and *tapeinòs* both translate into Hebrew as *'anî / 'anàw,* which means "poor" (cf. Ps 17:28; 24:9; 34:3, 19; etc.).[11]

---

11. For a deepening of this theme, see: S. Légasse, *Jésus et l'enfant. "Enfants," "petits" et "simples" dans la tradition synoptique* (Paris: Gabalda, 1969), especially 223–224, 243–244; and Deutsch, *Hidden Wisdom.*

If Matthew is the only one in the New Testament who combines the two terms, he is not the first to do so. In fact, we already find the phrase in the Greek version of Wisdom 3:12 (said "of the restored Jerusalem"): "I will leave in your midst a people meek and poor/humble [*prayn kài tapeinòn*]," and that of Isaiah 26:6 (said of the proud whom God had punished): "The foot tramples it, the feet of the poor, the steps of the needy [*praèòn kài tapeinôn*]." Our evangelist therefore takes it up again and applies to Jesus this passage and the idea behind it, showing how the Master is at the same time the ideal type and the leader of a people who are "the meek and poor of the Lord." To the ancient expression Matthew only adds "of heart," to underline an aspect very dear to him: the interior and spiritual dimension of poverty, or rather, humility. But what concretely does this "humility of heart" mean?

The following passage illustrates it well. Our evangelist shows the Master's meekness before his disciples and their accusers (12:1–21). While the Pharisees with their rigorous interpretation of the Law load the people with insupportable burdens, Jesus shows himself the interpreter of the divine mercy. Not by chance in 12:7 do we find for the second time on the lips of Jesus the citation of Hosea 6:6: "It is mercy I want and not sacrifice" (cf. 9:13).

Finally, the attitude of meek benevolence shines through in the healing of the man with the paralyzed hand (12:9–14). Jesus' accusers, indignant at the invalid's healing on the Sabbath, decide to eliminate Jesus, but he takes care of all those who are following him and heals them (12:15).

Here is the true picture of the Servant of the Lord! Matthew sees fulfilled in Jesus the prophetic passage that presents the Messiah filled with goodness and meekness, far removed from every form of violence and careful not to extinguish the burning wick (in 12:18–21, Matthew extensively cites Isaiah 42:1–4). We are given proof and advance indication of the supreme demonstration of meekness Jesus will display in his passion.

In biblical tradition meekness and humility are connected to the ideal of the wise person and especially to the figure of Moses. The Book of Numbers describes him as "very humble, more so than anyone else on the face of the earth" (Num 12:3). Yet he rebelled against Pharaoh and guided a rebellious people toward freedom! It is to his meekness (*'anawàh*) that Judaic tradition attributes the great intimacy accorded him by God, the fact, that is, that Moses could enter into the cloud of glory (*Mekilta de-Rabbi Ishmael*, 9:98–117).

The icon of Jesus "meek and humble of heart" depicts attitudes of interior strength and not weakness, as a culture of violence and power would tend to see it. Jesus' meekness is a strength of freedom that rises up against the keepers of an order only "officially" religious, to tear away the yoke of human prescriptions elevated to divine norms.

The freedom Christ offers to the oppressed certainly doesn't mean a freedom without rules, but the Law is freed because it includes a new relationship with God. Joyous experience of the divine paternity is what makes the "yoke" sweet and light. The Abba-Father, from whom the son

Jesus receives everything, does not place on humanity an oppressive yoke. Unlike many rabbis who burden the shoulders of their followers with norms and precepts, the Master of the meek and humble heart has pity on those crippled beneath a load that is too heavy. The compassionate Master and Shepherd promises "rest" that is "peace" (the rest of the true "Sabbath," of which the Letter to the Hebrews speaks in 4:9). Such rest comes to the one who willingly accepts Jesus' "yoke."[12]

Yet the contrary impression remains. The Master has compassion on all those who are weary and carry heavy burdens, but he also doesn't seem to give them a break: they still have to carry a "yoke."[13] Therefore the consolation lies entirely in the difference between the yokes, in the fact that "his" is declared "light and easy." Is that because it is relieved of the weight of pharisaic interpretation? Undoubtedly, but not only this. Christ's yoke is light primarily because he himself intends to carry it with us, making himself not only our Master but also our "partner." He is the one who shares our yoke (from the Latin *cum-iugo* = "with/under the same yoke"). A fate shared is lighter to carry, above all if Jesus is the "partner."

This Christ is therefore our *partner* as long as one condition remains firm: that we take seriously the invitation to

12. Cf. E. Bosetti, "Alla scuola di Gesù, il 'povero di Jahweh' (Mt 11:28–30)," *Parole di Vita* 38 (1993), 174–185; E. López Fernández, "El yugo de Jesús (Mt 11:28–30). Historia y sentido de una metáfora," *StudOvet* 11 (1983), 65–118.

13. The image of the yoke evokes the cross, which the disciple of Christ must be ready to carry (16:24).

learn from him who is meek and humble of heart. Biblical tradition requires that animals under the pole and bolt of the yoke be of the same race. It is illegal for the Levite to put animals that are different—for example, a donkey and an ox—under the same yoke![14] Outside the metaphor, it is necessary to learn from Christ in order to experience his support as the partner who carries the yoke with us.

Dialoguing with the Word

- Place yourself at the feet of Jesus, the Master who is meek of heart. Ask him to give you the "rest" that he promised to those who come to him with faith. Lay before his loving gaze all that anguishes and preoccupies you: anxieties, worries, fears...

- Ask Jesus to help you to understand what oppresses your life, what is your heavy "yoke" of which he wants to free you. Let him fully enter your life, including your decisions and preoccupations, as the friend who wants to carry the yoke with you.

---

14. "You shall not plow with an ox and a donkey yoked together" (Deut 22:10); cf. Lev 19:19. Based on this directive, Paul exhorts the Corinthians not to allow themselves "to be mismatched with unbelievers" (2 Cor 6:14).

CHAPTER SEVEN

"From then on, Jesus..."

Way of the cross and of the Church

(Matthew 16–18)

W e will take a bird's-eye view of the second part of Matthew's Gospel, which we could refer to as "the revelation of the hidden mystery" (16:21–28:20). What comes into view is the suffering of the Christ and the necessity of following him along the way that leads to Jerusalem, where hope crosses the Passover of death and resurrection. We will stop in particular at the announcements of the passion and the reactions of Peter (16:21–17:27), and on the communitarian discourse (18:1–35). More than Mark and Luke, Matthew reserves a place in the foreground for the Apostle Peter and his reactions. We see him intervene three times: in connection to the first two announcements of the passion and in the context of the discourse on the Church.

Revelations and temptations

We find ourselves at Caesarea Philippi, near the northern frontier of the Holy Land, before enchanting scenery that features the slopes of Mount Hermon and the flowing rivers of the Jordan. In this framework the Master opens an investigation into his identity. He speaks of a mysterious appointment of himself as "Son of Man,"[1] and asks a question that demands an answer:

> When Jesus came to the district of Caesarea Philippi he began to question his disciples, "Who do men say the Son of Man is?" (16:13)

The disciples recount what has been said, a survey of public opinion offering four trends that converge in calling Jesus a "prophet." In Herod's circle Jesus was identified with the Baptist;[2] elsewhere people were mentioning the names of two significant prophets, Elijah and Jeremiah;[3] others said more generally that he was a prophet:

---

1. Already in use in religious writing of the time, in the Gospel the title "Son of Man" always and only appears on the lips of Jesus. In Matthew it recurs thirty times, first in 8:20 and then throughout the account. On the self-appointment of Jesus as Son of Man, see Kingsbury, *Matteo. Un racconto,* in particular chapter 5; in addition, H. Shürmann, "Observations on the Son of Man Title in the Speach Source. Its Occurrence in Closing and Introductory Expressions," in *The Shape of Q. Signal Essays on the Sayings Gospel,* by J.S. Kloppenborg (Minneapolis: Fortress Press, 1994), 74–97.

2. King Herod Antipas, hearing of Jesus' fame, said: "This is John the Baptist; he has been raised from the dead" (Mt 14:1–2).

3. Jeremiah's name does not appear in the parallel passages of Mark and Luke. Only Matthew mentions it, and I think it is because Jeremiah shares a similar destiny with Jesus.

"Some say John the Baptist," they said, "others, Elijah, still others, Jeremiah or one of the prophets" (16:14).

The Master presses: "But who do you say that I am?" The question challenges each one directly. I imagine a moment of silence and then Peter's voice, clear as water springing from a fountain:

"You are the Messiah, the Son of the Living God!" (16:16)

Jesus' answer

Unlike in Mark and Luke, in Matthew Jesus reacts to the confession of Peter by declaring him "blessed," with words that seem to be a confession in their turn, according to a logic of reciprocity:

"Blessed are you, Simon bar Jonah, for it was not flesh and blood that revealed this to you, but my Father in heaven. And now I tell you that you are Peter, and on this rock I will build my church, and the gates of hell will not prevail against it. I will give you the keys to the kingdom of heaven, and whatever you bind on earth will have been bound in heaven, and whatever you loose on earth will have been loosed in heaven" (16:17–19).

Jesus declares Simon bar Jonah, "the son of Jonah," *makàrios,* "blessed"—a word that recalls the Beatitudes (5:3–12). The Master rejoices because the Father hides the mystery from the wise and reveals it to little ones (11:25). Simon bar Jonah (the name calling to mind the prophet Jonah, who was sent in spite of himself to preach mercy to the pagans of Nineveh) has intuited this not because he is sharper or more intelligent than the others, but because of the gratuitous revelation of the Father. It is to the little ones that the Father is pleased to reveal the mystery.

This theme of hiddenness and revelation plays an important role in Matthew's account. It is also the hermeneutic key used for the parables, especially the central one, where the Master offers "things hidden from the foundation of the world" (13:35; Ps 78:2). "To you [the disciples] has been granted to understand the mysteries of the kingdom of heaven, but to them [the crowds] it is not granted." The allusion to the "game" God is playing is clear, even though the verb "to reveal" (*apokalyptô*) is not used. Matthew seems to strategically reserve it, keeping it for Peter's confession. Although completely absent in Mark, this verb is dear to Matthew, who uses it four times in the discourse on mission (10:26), then twice more in the hymn of jubilation (11:25, 27), and finally again in the response to Peter: "It was not flesh or blood that revealed this to you, but my Father in heaven" (16:17). The confession of faith is a gift of the Father who reveals Christ to the little ones.

And from this same position of revelatory gift, Jesus repeats to Simon: *You have said who I am for you, and I say who you are for me. You are Peter* (the Greek translation of the Aramaic name *Kepha,* "rock") *and on your rock-like faith I will build my Church.*[4]

---

4. Jesus promises Peter the power to "bind and to loose," an expression which in Judaism means to prohibit or to permit, and, when all is said and done, to exclude or to readmit into the religious community.

To go to Jerusalem and suffer much

What is striking within this framework in which the evangelist sets the way of the cross and of the Church is Peter's instability. Being declared "blessed" does not stop him from immediately receiving the title of *satan*. Peter is not guaranteed from falling into a *satanic* attitude opposed to the revelation of the Father and to the mission of Christ.

Matthew 16:21 illustrates a turning point. The evangelist points out the change of situation with a formula present only one other time: in 4:17, where the kerygmatic activity, the announcement of the Master, is introduced:

Mt 4:17: "From that time on Jesus began *to preach*
          [*kêryssein*]"
Mt 16:21: "From then on Jesus began *to explain*
          [*deiknyein*]"

This double "from then on" (*apò tòte*) articulates the story in two large sections, which deal with the preaching of the Kingdom (4:17—16:20) and the progressive manifestation of the way of the cross (16:21—28:20). These are two decisive turning points; the first takes place when Jesus leaves Nazareth and moves to Capernaum; the second, after Caesarea Philippi, when he begins to say *openly* that he must go up to Jerusalem and suffer much. Scripture scholars refer to this turning point as the "Galilean crisis." It is not yet the beginning of the journey (which will take place in Matthew 19),[5] but the announcement of

---

5. According to the fourth evangelist, Jesus goes to Jerusalem at different times: on the occasion of the Passover and for other feasts. Not so for the synoptic evangelists, for whom the Master goes up to Jerusalem only once during his public life and finds death.

what it signifies and implies for one who wants to follow the Christ. In short, it is not enough to preach and work miracles. One must follow to the very end the path of shared love, and this love inevitably takes the form of the *way of the cross.*

The discourse on the Church is placed in this setting of the cross, already scandalous for the first of the apostles. Matthew insists more than the others on the figure of Peter. Whether in the first or second announcement of the passion, they are accompanied by episodes in which he is seen as the protagonist:

> From then on Jesus began to explain to his disciples that he had to go on to Jerusalem and suffer terrible things at the hands of the elders and chief priests and scribes and be put to death and rise on the third day. Peter took him aside and began to remonstrate with him, saying, "God be merciful to you, Lord. This will never happen to you." But Jesus turned to Peter and said, "Get behind me, Satan! You are an occasion of sin for me—you are not thinking the thoughts of God but of men!" (16:21–23)

This passage expresses *concisely* what we proclaim in the Creed: "...he suffered under Pontius Pilate, died, and was buried, and on the third day rose again from the dead"—the nucleus of our Christological faith.

But did Jesus already know that he would rise *on the third day?*[6] If we answer yes because he was God and thus

---

6. The three days Jesus spent in the sepulcher are equivalent to a few hours on Friday (the *Parasceve*), to the whole of Saturday, and to the beginning of the third day, the first day after the Sabbath. For the Bible, the day begins with vespers of the preceding day. But the expression "third day" is not to be understood only in the temporal sense.

knew everything, then the problem is resolved before it is
even understood. However, the text leaves room for a less
detailed treatment of the subject. The expression "the third
day" alludes to the text of the prophet Hosea: "After two
days he will revive us; on the third day he will raise us up"
(Hos 6:2). What could the disciples have understood from
this allusion? Jewish Scripture scholars interpret this text
of Hosea from the perspective of the resurrection of the
just at the end of time,[7] and most likely the disciples also
understood it in this way. It makes the following narrative
more understandable, beginning with the reaction of
Peter, who undoubtedly believed in the resurrection of the
just but rebelled at a course of humiliation and suffering.
So he takes the Master aside and, half dismayed and half
horrified, tells him: "God be merciful to you, Lord. This
will never happen to you."

Peter must have felt responsible for the group, and in
particular for Jesus, who was a guest in his house at Capernaum. But the Master's response is decisive: *hypage opìsô
mou, satanà,* "Get behind me, Satan." The Peter to whom
the revelation of the Father was addressed now takes on
the satanic role of the tempter. He is a stumbling block on
the way of obedience.

Jesus reacts by affirming his total adhesion to the
Father. *I have called you to* follow after me (4:19) *and not in
front of me,* the Master seems to say to the disciple who

---

7. At the time of Jesus, belief in the resurrection of the dead was pretty
widespread in Judaism, but found resistance among the Sadducees, a
Jewish religious group often named together with the Pharisees.

presumes to teach him the way. *You are a scandal to me because you do not understand the things of God.* The demand to avoid the scandal of the cross is typically worldly, opposed to the divine plan; it favors Satan, who is hostile to the mission of the Christ.

Therefore Jesus does not hesitate to blame whoever draws him away from obedience to the Father. Not only this, but he calls the whole group of disciples to himself and reaffirms that there is no other way for the one who wants to follow him:

> "Whoever would be my disciple must deny himself, he must take up his cross and follow me" (16:24).

There is no discipleship without sharing in the *way of the cross* walked by Christ. A disciple, in fact, is one who follows the Master and his destiny. "Take up your own cross" alludes to the crossbeam that the condemned carried right to the place of execution. In other words, Christian love accepts carrying the burden and suffering that come from the choice of justice according to God. Love that liberates carries its own cross and those of others—not with a long face, but with the serene expression of one who believes that on the "third day" Christ is risen and has conquered death forever.

Dialoguing with the Word

- Stop for a moment to deepen in prayer this Gospel passage. There is no more disturbing question for the Christian conscience than that asked by the Master

> at Caesarea Philippi: "And you, who do you say that I am?" Who is Jesus for you? Are you ready to confess him with the faith of Peter and to follow him along the way of the cross?
>
> • Renew with humility and faith, but also with all the strength of your heart, your adhesion to Jesus and the duty of following him on the way of the cross.

To save one's life for eternity

The text continues with a triple argument found also in Mark and Luke, a triple "for" (*gar*) centered on the word "life." This is about the most precious good that is offered to men: life in all its fullness, beyond historical horizons.

> "*For* whoever would save his life will lose it, while whoever loses his life for my sake will find it. *For* what good would it do a man to gain the whole world, but forfeit his life? Or what could a man give in exchange for his life? *For* the Son of Man will come in the glory of his Father with his angels, and then he will pay each according to their work" (16:25–27).

It is easy to let ourselves be seduced by material goods and by success, as if life depended on their attainment. But life is simply not within the power of man, of doctors or of medicine. To follow Jesus is to save one's life for eternity, since "the Son of Man will come in the glory of his Father and will repay each according to their work" (16:27).

> The eschatological perspective is affirmed here as absolutely fundamental for the believer, that is, what concerns the end

of the world and the coming in all its fullness of the Kingdom of God. We haven't heard of this for some time. However, even Paul tells us that, if there was nothing beyond this life, believers, no matter how much they delude themselves to the contrary, would be the most miserable of all (1 Cor 15:19). Christian salvation has become a paradox: only in losing our life, crucified as Jesus Christ, will we save it in him. Only thus will we be restored to peace, in the glory of tenderness, when his day will come.[8]

Jesus and Peter again

Matthew introduces the second announcement of the passion with an editorial nuance. The disciples "are gathered together" (*systrephomènôn*)[9] tightly around their Master, as if they foresee coming dangers.

> While they were together in Galilee Jesus told them, "The Son of Man is going to be handed over into the hands of men, and they will put him to death, but on the third day he will rise." And they were terribly distressed (17:22–23).

This second announcement does not speak of Jerusalem or the Jewish authorities. Primarily it seems to reinforce the psychological aspect, as a kind of anticipation of the anguish that will become apparent at Gethsemane. We are still moving about Galilee but with a different spirit,

---

8. S. Quinzio, *I Vangeli della Domenica* (Milan: Adelphi, 1998), 129.

9. *Systrèphô* is a very rare verb, appearing only twice in the New Testament. In the Greek version of the Septuagint, it often means "to gather together against someone, to conspire" (2 Sam 15:31; 1 Kings 16:9; etc.). It seems to be chosen here precisely to reflect the feeling of danger that spread through the group of disciples.

marked by an awareness of a coming end that has the taste of betrayal: "The Son of Man will be handed over/ betrayed (*paradidosthai*)."

We are therefore invited to enter into the psyche and soul of Jesus, also in his self-appointment as the "Son of Man," a title that combines the aspects of humiliation and glory. On one hand, Jesus introduces the title in strict connection with his suffering (as usual, we also find it in the other two synoptics' announcements of the passion); on the other hand, it recalls the apocalyptic vision of Daniel, where the Son of Man receives power, glory, and kingship (Dn 7:9–14; cf. Mt 26:64). Therefore it is a suffering open to the future of God, as attested by the three remaining announcements of the passion and death, which include the resurrection. In any case, the disciples are stuck on the first dimension, because of which "they were terribly distressed" (17:22).

And so, in connection with the second announcement, Matthew (and only he) refers to an episode that again revolves around the figure of Peter:[10]

> When they came to Capernaum those who were collecting the temple tax came up to Peter and said, "Does not your teacher pay the temple tax?" "Certainly he does!" he said (17:24–25).

---

10. As Tassin rightly notes (*Vangelo di Matteo*, 211), Peter, "the future head of the Church, is [the one] who argues with the Master on delicate questions (as he already does, by the way, in the rites of ablution in Mt 15:15), and it is on his testimony that the conduct to be followed will be decided."

Every Jew was yearly required to give two drachmas or a half-shekel of silver for the expenses of temple worship. Peter has no doubt that his Master will pay the established tax like everyone else. But coming into the house, Jesus heads him off with an objection:

> "What do you think, Simon? The kings of the earth—from whom do they collect tax or toll? From their followers or from others?" When Peter said, "From others," Jesus said to him, "So then their followers are exempt. But so we do not offend them, go to the sea, cast a hook in, and take the first fish that comes up, and when you open its mouth you will find a silver coin, worth twice the temple tax; take it and give it to them for me and you" (17:25–27).

The Master claims first of all to be exempt from the tax. These are imposed on servants and citizens, not on sons! And Peter, who has confessed that Jesus is "the Son of the living God," cannot but agree. So the Master affirms his freedom as Son in regard to the Temple and the Law. But with a certain *humor* he abides by the rules of the game.

Today restaurants in Tiberius include on their menu "the fish of St. Peter," a name derived from the present episode. Undoubtedly, the fish Peter catches with the silver coin in its mouth has the flavor of folklore, but the importance of the message goes well beyond it and is in perfect keeping with the theological perspective of Matthew's Jesus, who observes and fulfills the Law. Perhaps at the time of editing the Gospel, the episode could also have meant something else; although Jewish Christians would know themselves to be sons and daughters, they would continue just the same to pay the temple tax, in solidarity with their people.[11]

And so the miracle of the fish introduces the discourse on the Church, where Peter again enters the scene with an intriguing question: "Lord, how many times can my brother sin against me and I will have to forgive him?" (18:21).

The discourse on the Church

It is certainly not a treatise in ecclesiology, much less in canon law! In this discourse, the fourth, Matthew proposes certain essential features regarding the style of life and fundamental orientations for the community of Jesus.

How did the Master imagine his Church? What did he put in the first place, and what attitudes did he inculcate?

What clearly emerges is that the Church is not an autonomous undertaking, having a purpose or aim in itself, but is a community directed to the Kingdom. It is a community of brothers and sisters searching for the will of the Father (12:50), and therefore completely at the service of the divine plan of salvation.

One notices different connections with the discourse on mission; both are directed to the group of disciples. Let's take a look at the literary composition of Matthew 18.

---

11. Analogously, Paul claims the freedom to eat any kind of food, even meat sacrificed to idols he knew well to be nothing. But he immediately adds that if this were to scandalize his brothers, he would never eat meat again (1 Cor 8:13).

Three questions and three parables

The discourse is carefully composed, based on a symmetrical outline showing the ecclesial themes our evangelist has most at heart. It is articulated in three questions, addressed respectively to the disciples, to Jesus, and to Peter.

In the beginning, the disciples ask the crucial question that sets the tone for the discourse: "Who is the greatest in the kingdom of heaven?"(18:1). Jesus instead asks a question with the purpose of *involving* his listeners in the parable of the Good Shepherd: "What do you think?" (18:12). The third question comes from the mouth of Peter: "How many times should I forgive my *brother,* as many as *seven* times?" (18:21).

These *three questions* already provide an initial articulation of the text, but that is not their only distinguishing feature. Another significant aspect is that the answers are provided through *parables:* the first in the form of action (a child placed in the midst of them), the other two in narrative form. Certain sayings of the Master, artfully distributed, allow the discourse to go forward under a lexical and thematic profile: from the word "child," used in a real sense (*paidìon,* vv. 1–5), we go to the expression "these little ones" (*mikròi toùtoi,* vv. 6–14), and then to the words "brother" (*adelphòs*) and "church" (*ekklêsìa,* vv. 15–35).[12] These elements suggest articulating the discourse in three sections:

12. The reading is divided this way: *child/children* four times in vv. 1–5; *"these little ones"* three times in vv. 6, 10, 14; *brother* four times in vv. 15–35; *church* two times in v. 17. One recalls that in the Gospels the term *ekklêsìa* is present only in Matthew, four times in all.

1. THE GREATEST IN THE KINGDOM (18:1–5)

> **Question:** *Who is the greatest?*
> **Parable:** at the center, the CHILD!
> > — if you do not become as CHILDREN...
> > — whoever accepts a CHILD in my name...

2. PASTORAL ATTENTION TO THE LITTLE ONES
   (18:6–14)

> > — if anyone *scandalizes* one of THESE LITTLE ONES...
> > — be careful not to despise one of THESE LITTLE
> > ONES...
> **Question:** *What do you think?*
> **Parable:** the good shepherd and the lost sheep
> ...that not one of THESE LITTLE ONES should be lost!

3. FRATERNAL CORRECTION AND FORGIVENESS
   (18:15–35)

> > — if your BROTHER sins against you, go and point it
> > out to him...
> **Question:** *How many times should I forgive my* BROTHER?
> **Parable:** the generous king and the unforgiving servant
> ...unless each of you forgives his BROTHER from his heart.

In the first section, the canons of greatness at use in society (then and now) are turned upside down: the greatest in the Kingdom is the one who humbles himself (*tapeinôsei*). Jesus responds to the disciples' question with an eloquent gesture, placing a child "in their midst." And then he explains the lesson: If "you do not convert yourselves" from your pretensions of greatness and become *like children*, you will not "enter the kingdom of heaven."

On the basis of this reversal, the second section focuses on the "little ones" of the community, while the third section reminds us of the need for fraternal correction, for forgiveness, and for communitarian prayer.

Who is the greatest?

Matthew silently passes over the origin of this earthly argument among the disciples, as a glance at the parallel passage in Mark's Gospel shows. It presents a question that sounds almost spontaneous and is about the "kingdom of heaven." This he allows to be framed immediately within the discourse of the Church in the proper perspective, precisely that of the Kingdom.

Reading the synoptics (Mt 18:1–5 and Mk 9:33–37) puts us in touch with a different perspective:[13]

Mt 18:1–5	*Mk 9:33–37*
	Then they came to Capernaum. When he was inside the house he asked them, "What were you arguing about on the way?"
At that time the disciples came to Jesus and said, "Who is the greatest in the kingdom of heaven?"	But they were silent, because on the way they had been arguing among themselves about who was the most important.

---

13. The argument is noted also in Luke, who points it out twice, after the second announcement of the passion and in the context of the last supper: cf. Lk 9:46–48 and 22:24–27.

He sat down and called the
Twelve and said to them,
"If anyone wishes to be first,
he must be the last of all
and the servant of all."

He called a child forward,
stood it before them,
and said:

Then he took a child
and stood it before them,
and he put his arms around it
and said to them,

"Amen I say to you, unless
you turn about and become
like children, you will not ever
enter the kingdom of heaven.

Therefore, whoever humbles
himself like this child,
he is the greatest
in the kingdom of heaven.

And whoever receives
one such child in my name,
receives me."

"Whoever receives
one such child in my name
receives me;
and whoever receives me,
receives not me
but the One who sent me."

As we already know, in the Gospel of Matthew the term "kingdom of heaven" means the "reign of God." From this perspective, the disciples' question does not seem to be merely ambitious, but also decisive. In the end, what is important in the Kingdom of heaven? How will the heavenly Father judge things? Who is the "greatest" in his eyes?

Jesus, who in another place describes himself personally as the Way (Jn 14:7), does not give a detailed academic analysis or respond with a treatise on perfection, but concretely shows the disconcerting hierarchy of greatness in God's eyes; "the greatest" is the one who freely and willingly becomes "the smallest." The Kingdom of heaven initiated on earth inaugurates a new way of establishing relationships—a way made visible in Jesus. It is a manner of living together characterized above all by humility—a humility that is not *optional,* but is an indispensable attitude in the Christian community.

"Who is the greatest?" In light of Mark's account, such a question lets us understand how the biggest temptation in the Church is the desire for power. Jesus repeatedly had to oppose in his disciples the ambition to be the first (cf. Mk 10:35–45; Mt 20:20–28; Lk 22:24–27; Jn 13:12–14).

Putting a child at the center—*in the middle* of the circle of disciples—Jesus challenges them and us to change our way of living. It is a strong call to conversion: to become like children who trust their father. This does not mean infantilism, but freely choosing the submission and humility that at the time of Jesus and in all of ancient society were the obligatory prerogative of children.

The child is *in the midst,* at the center of attention, but not in today's mode of media publicity or of sexual tourism.[14] At the time of Jesus, children had no rights. Along with women and slaves, they belonged to the so-

---

14. Cf. P. Monni, *L'arcipelago della Vergogna: Turismo sessuale e pedofilia* (Rome: Edizioni Universitarie Romane, 2001).

called "weak category" and were considered their parents'
possession. They had no right to speak and so could not
object; they had to obey, and that was it. Schoolmasters
had full license to punish and beat them; the *paideia*, that
is, education, was imparted to the sound of the whip![15]

Jesus, who used the image of "capricious children" to
describe his generation (11:16–17), says nothing here
about the qualities of the child, whether good or naughty.
He puts a child at the center as the standard of greatness.
It is not a question of imitating the child, but of "convert-
ing oneself" and becoming "like" children (*hos ta paidìa*) in
the hands of God.

In other words, greatness in the Kingdom of heaven is
measured by unconditional trust, which guided Jesus'
entire life. It is an attitude in distinct contrast with the subtle and ever recurring temptation to be God Almighty.

Jesus encourages us to change our way of seeing, both
personally and as a Church. His community is not an effi-
cient enterprise where the more one takes on and distin-
guishes oneself, the more that person advances, right to
the highest level. The disciples have to remember this.
Introducing the discourse on mission, Jesus noted that the
harvest was great but the laborers few. Yet he did not
encourage the Church to be the protagonist; rather, he

---

15. St. Augustine also notes: "Our parents laughed at the punishments
inflicted on us children by the teachers.... We loved to play, and we were
punished by adults who nonetheless did the same themselves. But where-
as the frivolous pursuits of grown-up people are called 'business,' children
are punished for behaving in the same fashion" (*The Confessions*, I, 9:15).

encouraged the intensification of prayer (9:37–38). In short, the "greatest" is not the one who commands or does more, but the one who is completely abandoned to the Father like Jesus. Here is the child placed at the center![16]

Be careful that you do not despise these little ones

From "the child" Matthew proceeds to "the little ones" (18:6–14), a term that connects both sections together in thematic unity. In fact, we find it at the conclusion of the parable of the Good Shepherd, where Matthew remembers the will of the Father that not one of "these little ones" should be lost.

The figure of the child evokes the "little ones" in a metaphoric sense. This expression takes in all those who, for different reasons, are not sufficiently grown. One could think of the neophyte, the disciple in formation who is not yet adult in his or her faith; or of one who remains somewhat fragile even after he or she has received the sacraments of Christian initiation. We need to give particular attention to these little ones. We need to be like the Good Shepherd, who goes out immediately in search of them.

The first part of Jesus' teaching touches on the seriousness of scandal. The Lord realistically admits that there will always be scandals, yet he also expresses severe condemnation:

---

16. Jesus' feeling regarding children continues in 19:13–15. "Let the children be, and do not stop them from coming to me, for to such as these belongs the kingdom of heaven!" says the Master to the disciples who were rebuking them.

"But whoever causes one of these little ones who believe in me to sin, it would be better for him to have a donkey's millstone hung around his neck and be sunk in the depths of the sea. Woe to the world because of occasions of sin! It is inevitable that occasions of sin should come, yet woe to the man through whom the occasion of sin comes! If your hand or your foot causes you to sin, cut it off and throw it away from you! It is better for you to enter life crippled or lame, than to have two hands or two feet and be thrown into eternal fire. And if your eye causes you to sin, pluck it out and throw it away from you! It is better for you to enter life one-eyed, than to have two eyes and be thrown into the fire of Gehenna. See that you do not look down on one of these little ones, for I tell you, their angels in heaven continually look upon the face of my Father in heaven" (18:6–10).

Certain phrases return that were already heard in the Sermon on the Mount: it is better to enter eternal life deprived of one part of ourselves, like our hands, feet, or even eyes, than to not enter it at all (18:8–9; cf. 5:29–30). Hand and foot are symbolic of action; the eye, of intention. Scandals are removed starting with ourselves, with taking away the beam from our eye before we remove the splinter from the eye of another. Community is not constructed without personal asceticism.[17]

---

17. In the First Letter to the Corinthians, which preceded the writing of Matthew's Gospel, St. Paul speaks of the Church as a body with different members and functions; a mystical and social body (cf. 1 Cor 12:12–27). In this perspective one could thus interpret: "If your foot [that is, your brother] is an occasion of scandal for you...cut it [him] off"! And you would thus have the so-called practice of excommunication applied by Paul himself in the case of incest: "The perpetrator of this deed should be removed from among you!" (1 Cor 5:2).

Verse 10 goes from the danger of *scandal* to that of *despising*. Precisely because they are the little ones, these believers are defended and particularly loved. The community should be careful not to "look down on them," and should express in their regard the care of which the parable speaks (vv. 12–14). Not only must one be careful not to cause the fall of one of these *little ones* with "scandal," one must also overcome the temptation of watching them from a distance, with a mixture of pity and disdain. There should be no barriers or distrust among believers! One should not close oneself up in a comfortable elitism, in small political groups according to social classes and levels of instruction. The *little ones* are to be placed in the center of the loving interest of the community, as Jesus has concretely done with the child.

This theme is particularly dear to our evangelist, who returns to it even in the last discourse on the end times. When the Son of Man will come in his glory and take his place on the throne of judgment, the determining criteria for one's eternal destiny will be precisely what one has done (or not done) "to one of the least." This is because Christ considers them "brothers" and deems as done to him what is done to them (cf. 25:31–46).

What do you think?

"What do you think? If a man has a hundred sheep and one of them strays away, will he not leave the ninety-nine on the mountainside and go look for the one that went astray? And if he happens to find it, amen, I say to you, he rejoices over it more than over the ninety-nine that did not go

astray. Likewise, it is not the will of your Father in heaven
that one of these little ones should be lost" (18:12–14).

Matthew introduces the parable of the Good Shepherd
with a question: "What do you think?" This is a question
pastors of the Church should learn to ask, since it draws
others into the discussion, encourages dialogue, and elicits
reactions. A dictator will never ask such a question.
Neither will one who is afraid of losing control of a situation. But Jesus, a free man, is not afraid of such provoking
questions: "If a man has a hundred sheep and one of them
strays away, will he not leave the ninety-nine on the
mountainside and go look for the one that went astray?"
Thus a new question extends the first.

Naturally the one who asks a question expects a
response. Jesus, too, awaits our answer at the end of the
story. Do you agree with his point of view, with his absurd
logic? It is not at all obvious what the shepherd of the
story is doing. He risks losing the entire flock to run after
one little sheep! Jesus, however, seems to suppose that
everyone agrees with his point of view. And he can then
draw the conclusion that takes us "beyond": "Likewise, it
is not the will of your Father in heaven that one of these
little ones should be lost" (v. 14).

What does this conclusion mean? Above all, it underscores a relationship of similarity (*houtos*) between the shepherd's behavior and God's. Like the shepherd, who is not
resigned to the loss of his sheep, so God is with regard to his
children. The story establishes a clear correspondence
between the lost sheep and the condition of the "little ones."

In the parable, the sheep that is "lost" seems to be valued—paradoxically—more than the other ninety-nine, from the moment in which the shepherd was ready to "leave them" in order to find the one. If then he finds it, the joy that he has for this little sheep is greater than the contentment that comes from having the ninety-nine safe. All of this says how important that sheep is to the shepherd.

But the conclusion is not satisfied with establishing the relationship between the person in the parable and the behavior of God, our merciful and good Father. Echoes of it can be found in the ecclesial context of chapter 18, and thus the point is to illustrate behavior within the community. In the lost sheep, Matthew seems to see one of the little ones belonging to the Christian community,[18] who is not "lost" but has "strayed." For various reasons that person has distanced and marginalized himself or herself, and the duty of the shepherd, of the one who has responsibility in the Church, is therefore to go and search for that person with as much care as possible. And he rejoices if he is able to find this little one, according to the saving will of the Father.

All of this is in thematic continuity with the rest of the ecclesial discourse: "If your brother should sin against you,

---

18. The parable of the lost sheep is noted also in the *Gospel of Thomas* (Coptic Apocrypha), with different variations that notably depart from the evangelical meaning. The sheep who is lost is "the largest," and when the shepherd reaches it he says: "I love you more than the other ninety-nine!" (I, 107). We are dealing here with the most beautiful and healthy sheep, which explains the shepherd's predilection for it. It is exactly the opposite in Matthew's Gospel, in which the smallest ones should be the object of particular care and concern.

go show him his error between you and him alone. If he listens to you, you have won your brother back" (18:15).

Two complementary perspectives

In the editing of Luke 15:3–7, the sheep is called "lost," in a life-or-death situation, while in Matthew it is seen as "strayed." In Luke's account the situation of the sheep is therefore worse, notwithstanding the evangelist's certainty that the shepherd will find it. In fact, he says, "and when he finds it" (Lk 15:5). The narration in Matthew, instead, seems more cautious: "if he succeeds in finding it." Although the sheep is described as *strayed* rather than *lost,* and therefore in a less serious situation, it still hangs on an "if," a reservation regarding the outcome of the search. It is not certain that the shepherd will find the sheep. If a wolf comes before he gets there, what will he find?

The parable, whether in Matthew's account or in Luke's, finds its inspiration in Ezekiel 34:1–16, the passage in which the prophet announces the Lord's severe judgment against the shepherds of Israel, who pasture themselves instead of the sheep (vv. 2–10). The shepherds are destroying not just any flock; it belongs to the Lord and is the object of his care and his efforts. Ezekiel declares that these shepherds have betrayed their duty. They are lacking in attention to the weak, the poor, and the needy. He denounces them for a series of omissions: "You have not strengthened the weak, you have not healed the sick, you have not bound up the injured, you have not brought back the strayed, you have not sought the lost..."

(Ezek 34:4). The shepherds' wickedness is countered by the pastoral work of God. He himself will shepherd his people. He will search for his sheep, heal them, and gather them from every place:

"I will seek the lost [*apólolòs*], and I will bring back the strayed [*planómenon*]" (Ezek 34:16).

This verse from Ezekiel is taken up again in the Gospel parable, whether in Matthew or in Luke's version. It is strange to note how, to describe the situation of the sheep, Matthew and Luke select respectively one of the two terms used in Ezekiel: the first, "strayed" (*planómenon*); the second, "lost" (*apólolòs*).

Caring for sinners, Jesus concretely shows the fulfillment of the prophecy. This is particularly explicit in Luke 15:1–3. The tax collectors and sinners are the sheep who are sick, scattered, and lost. They are treated harshly by the shepherds of Israel (the scribes and Pharisees), who avoid their company and want to "distance them" from the flock. Luke therefore prefers the Christological perspective, while Matthew the ecclesiological. But for both evangelists, Jesus reveals God's paternal care.

Fraternal correction and prayer

Jesus proposes a community of brothers who must learn to live together in truth and charity, offering the gifts of fraternal correction (vv. 15–18) and forgiveness (vv. 21–35). In the middle, as a bridge, our evangelist gathers two verses on the power of communitarian prayer (vv. 19–20). It is as if correction and forgiveness are enveloped by prayer, because what seems humanly impossible, or destined for failure, can be accomplished fruitfully in the name of Jesus:

> "Again I say to you, if two of you agree on earth about any matter they ask for, it will come to be for them through my Father in heaven. For where two or three are gathered in my name, I am there among them" (18:19–20).[19]

Don't skip the first step!

> "If your brother should sin against you, go show him his error between you and him alone. If he listens to you, you have won your brother back; but if he does not listen, take one or two others with you, so that every statement may stand on the testimony of two or three witnesses. If he refuses to listen to them, tell the church, but if he refuses to listen even to the church, regard him as you would a Gentile or a tax collector" (18:15–17).

The passage presents Jesus' teaching on a delicate theme that was fundamental for the life of the community. The practice of fraternal correction was not foreign in the biblical world, where it was seen as a gift from God and a duty for every brother or sister who lived within the community. But the pedagogy of God is not readily comprehended; people have a hard time understanding that "the Lord punishes those who are close to him" (Jdt 8:27).

---

19. Here Matthew seems to be adapting a Jewish phrase that says: "If two men find themselves together and the words of the law are in the midst of them [as the subject of their conversation], the presence of God [the *Shekinah*] is in the midst of them."

This is why the Scriptures underline the attitudes of love, mercy, forgiveness, and compassion, and not only of severity in God's relations toward his people. This will become the model that must animate relationships within the whole community.[20]

We have already seen that Matthew is not describing a perfect community, one immune from scandals or a lessening of charity. Even in the Church the good grain lives together with the weeds.... The disciples remain weak people of little faith, tempted by doubts, human ambitions, and the desire for power. Therefore, there is all the more reason to speak of "correction."

The method Jesus proposes is articulated in three moments: personal dialogue, dialogue between brothers, and finally awareness of the community. Everything presupposes a serious duty to reestablish unity and concord.

The first moment considers fraternal correction in the strictly private form and places the accent on the personal and relational aspect more than on the juridical. The goal is to help the brother who has sinned to recognize his fault and convert himself.

---

20. Such a principle was codified in Lev 19:17–18, which later on becomes the reference point for every correction: "You shall not hate in your heart anyone of your kin; you shall reprove your neighbor, or you will incur guilt yourself. You shall not take vengeance or bear a grudge against any of your people, but you shall love your neighbor as yourself: I am the Lord." On this argument, see: S. Tellan, "La correzione fraternal nella chiesa di Matteo (Mt 18:15–20)," a doctoral thesis for the Gregorian University, Rome 1991–92 (published in part: Verona, 1996).

If personal dialogue is refused, the next step is correction proposed together with other brothers.[21] This means two or three brothers of the community of faith, who accompany the person who has been offended and take an active part in his discreet attempt to admonish the sinner.

Only in the third moment is the Church called in with its full authority. Naturally, even at this level the sinner remains free to accept or refuse conversion. And only in the case of refusal is the Church's position described in the proverbial form: "regard him as you would a Gentile or a tax collector."

Therefore, the community of Jesus must behave above all as a true *fraternity,* an authentic community of brothers and sisters. The gift of fraternal correction is to be offered to everyone; it is not a matter of submission but of *interior freedom.* In fact, it is relatively easy to correct "little ones" or subordinates, while it is a greater risk to do so when the matter concerns someone in authority or one who holds a position of power. But it is precisely here that the "Pauline liberty" governing fraternal correction is manifested.[22]

---

21. One notes an allusion to the law of witnesses in Deut 19:15: "A single witness shall not suffice to convict a person of any crime or wrongdoing in connection with any offense that may be committed. Only on the evidence of two or three witnesses shall a charge be sustained." But Matthew's perspective is slightly removed from this, because here the witnesses do not participate in a juridical procedure, but rather in a friendly attempt to convince a brother of his error.

22. Paul corrects Peter to his face. Why? Certainly not because he is against Peter, but because the issue in question is the Gospel, and because "Peter was obviously in the wrong" (Gal 2:11).

Seventy times seven

> Then Peter came and said to him, "Lord, how many times can my brother sin against me and I will have to forgive him? Up to seven times?" Jesus said to him, "I do not say to you up to seven times, but instead up to seventy-seven times" (18:21–22).

Peter asks, "How many times?" He believes himself very generous and magnanimous in indicating the biblical *seven.* But Jesus does not consider the question in the same way; he does not limit the effusion of forgiveness: *seventy times seven!*

The expression recalls and reverses the saying of the violent Lamech, who bragged about his capacity for vengeance: "If Cain is avenged sevenfold, truly Lamech seventy-sevenfold" (Gen 4:24). Jesus, on the contrary, proposes *seventy times seven* for a love that forgives.

Dialoguing with the Word

- Matthew is not afraid to present a Church of sinners, called to live in reconciliation and forgiveness. He teaches us to resolve differences according to the method indicated by Jesus, beginning with personal relationships, where it is possible to encounter the other on a level of equality. It is here that the favorable occasion for the "salvation" of a brother or sister takes place. How do you live by this method indicated by Jesus?

- What kind of room does prayer have in your fraternal relationships? Only a praying community is able

> to practice fraternal correction in an efficacious
> manner: "If two of you on earth agree to ask for
> anything whatever, my Father who is in heaven will
> give it to them," says Jesus. One's brother or sister is
> a living sign of his presence.

A Church that loves

Let us jump forward—hopefully not in an arbitrary way—guided by what I said was the crux of the cross, that is, Matthew's trait of weaving together the subject of the Church with the announcement of the passion. With Matthew 26 we find ourselves in Jerusalem right before the passion.[23] At the beginning of this chapter, the proximity of the Passover is mentioned:

"You know that the Passover will be in two days, and the Son of Man will be handed over to be crucified" (26:2).

Only Matthew uses this language. His audience has not changed. The discourse on mission was directed to the disciples, as was the communitarian discourse. Now again we read, "Jesus said to his disciples." We should expect the disciples to be united with this kind of confidence. They still have Jesus for two more days.

What follows is a dramatic, extreme contrast. Jesus goes to Bethany, to the house of Simon—a leper whom he

---

23. Recall that the discourse on the Church (Mt 18) is inserted in a broader narrative section, which comprises three announcements of the passion and resurrection (cf. 16:21; 17:12; 17:22–23).

probably healed. A woman, whose name Matthew does not record, approaches Jesus with an alabaster jar of very precious perfumed oil, which she pours on his head while he reclines at table.

Seeing this, the disciples become indignant: *Why this waste? It could have been sold at a good price in order to give to the poor.* Yet, in two more days Jesus would no longer be with them! And the woman had not heard what the Master had said to his own. They knew; she did not. She had not been there but still sees, because one sees well who sees with the heart. She sees and understands and makes a special gesture, anointing Jesus' head.

Remember that Matthew is not Luke, for whom a sinner anointed Jesus with perfumed ointment, and not on the head but on the feet (Lk 7:36–50). For John, the woman is Mary of Bethany, sister of Martha and Lazarus, and she too pours her ointment on the feet of the Master (Jn 12:1–8). Matthew instead is similar to Mark, who also remains silent about the woman's name, but values her gesture, because it was quite another thing to pour perfumed oil on a person's head (Mk 14:3–9). To anoint the head has a strong symbolic meaning. One recalls the royal anointing of David by the prophet Samuel (1 Sam 16:1–13). Jesus is the consecrated one par excellence: priest, king, and prophet of his people. But, practically speaking, who has anointed him? Who has ever poured oil on his head? No one, if not a woman!

Scripture scholars are reluctant to see here the anointing of the consecrated one. For me, instead, this anointing on the part of a woman seems entirely appropriate, in line with Mary's unusual maternity. The story of Jesus is surprising from beginning to end.[24]

In one way, the disciples were right. This gesture on the woman's part was certainly extravagant. But such "waste" bespeaks the measure of her love, and casts a contrasting light on the disciples' petty, stingy reasoning. They know that in two days Jesus will be crucified, and yet here they argue about the "wasted" ointment that could have been sold and the money given to the poor. They don't realize that in this instance, the "poor one" is Jesus!

And Jesus, in fact, defends the woman:

> "Why are you bothering the woman? She has done a beautiful thing for me. For the poor you always have with you, but me you will not always have. When she poured this oil on my body she did it to prepare me for burial" (26:10–12).

She has anticipated that anointing which no woman will ever perform, since on the day after the Sabbath, the women who carry the aromatic oils to the sepulcher to anoint Jesus' body will discover that he is no longer there. Jesus, however, attaches to this gesture of love a promise of great importance:

> "Amen, I say to you, wherever this good news is proclaimed in the whole world, what she did will also be told in memory of her" (26:13).

---

24. For a deepening of the topic, see: E. Bosetti, "La donna nel Nuovo Testamento," in *La donna: memoria e attualità. Donna ed esperienza di Dio nei solchi della storia,* edited by L. Borriello, 2 vols. (Città del Vaticano: Libreria Editrice Vaticana, 2000), I, 46–117.

In memory of her. The phrase seems a negation, because, paradoxically, not even the woman's name will be remembered. However, a symbol emerges from the silence surrounding the woman's name. It is a little like what happened with the mountain: by leaving it anonymous, it becomes greatly evocative.

It is not her name but what *she has done* that will be remembered! This woman becomes a symbol of a Church that is *prophetic* because it is *loving*. And therefore it is one capable of seeing here and now, in the unrepeatable historical situation, what is meaningful and is worth being done with extreme gratuitousness.

Epilogue

"I am with you"
From the mountain to all peoples

We find ourselves on the mountain, a scene particularly dear to Matthew, listening to Jesus' final
words, to the testament of the Risen One to the Church
(Mt 28:16–20). And so we return to the page from which
we started, in the conviction that it constitutes a fundamental key to reading the theology of the first evangelist.

The appointment is of the greatest importance, because
it is the first and last encounter of the disciples with the
Risen Lord. In Mark, this event is promised but not narrated; it remains shrouded in the mysterious and disconcerting
silence of the women (Mk 16:7–8).[1] For Matthew, instead,

---

1. It is believed that the real conclusion to Mark is 16:8, with the
women's surprising silence. The appearances recounted in Mk 16:9–20 are
not part of the original writings, but were added from a very early century, probably to make up for the embarrassment of such a conclusion. On
this argument, see: R. Vignolo, "Un finale reticente: interpretazione nar-
rativa di Mc 16:8," *Rivista Biblica* 38 (1990), 129–189.

240

the Risen One reveals himself in his glory on the mountain of Galilee, and he send his disciples to all the nations, assuring them of his presence: "Behold, I will be with you all the days until the end of the age" (Mt 28:20).

On the portal, as in the apse of that splendid basilica reconstructed in Matthew, beneath the majestic figure of the *Pantocrator*, we read an identical motto: "I-am-with-you" (Mt 1:23; 28:20). Jesus is Emmanuel, the "God-with-us"—an irruption of eternity into time, the incarnation of God in history, the presence of the Risen One in his Church.

But let us approach the text once more to gather hidden riches from it. Matthew 28:16–20 is described in two scenes. In the first, the disciples are the protagonists; in the second, the Risen One is so.

FIRST SCENE: vv 16–17

But the eleven disciples went into Galilee
to the mountain Jesus had directed them to.
And when they saw him they worshiped him,
but some were doubtful.

SECOND SCENE: vv. 18–20

Jesus came to them and spoke to them saying,
"*All* authority in heaven and on earth
has been given to me.
Go, therefore, and MAKE DISCIPLES of *all* nations,
BAPTIZING them in the name of the Father
and of the Son and of the Holy Spirit,
and teach them to OBSERVE
all that I have commanded you
and, behold, I will be with you
all days until the end of the age."

The first scene unfolds in silence. It is not said *when* it happens, but *where:* in Galilee, on the mountain indicated by the Risen One. It is he who determines the place of encounter.[2] That mountain, traditionally identified as Tabor, remains mysterious in the text. And perhaps the evangelist is purposely silent regarding its name. In the course of the Gospel we have encountered many scenes that take place "on the mountain," anonymous as usual. Are they different mountains or the same one? It is almost as if one were symbolically superimposed on the other. On one high mountain, Jesus resists the third temptation and conquers Satan (4:8–10); from the mountain he proclaims the Beatitudes (5:1–12); on the mountain he passes the night in prayer (14:23), heals the lame and the blind (15:29–30), and is transfigured (17:1–10). There is no doubt that the scene of this solemn apparition of the Risen One recalls both Tabor and Mount Sinai. One can grasp the evocative connection between the conclusion of Matthew and the account of Moses' vocation and mission.[3]

---

2. A new element emerges here, which is absent in the mission entrusted to the women by the angels and then by Jesus himself: "Go quickly and tell his disciples that he goes ahead of you into Galilee; you will see him there" (Mt 28:7, 10).

3. The disciples who go to the mountain indicated by Jesus recall Moses who reaches the mountain of God, while the second scene is constructed respectively from the words of Yahweh and the Risen One. One notes that the brief discourse of the Risen Jesus presents the same structure as that placed in the mouth of Yahweh: a) in the first place, it is a word of revelation concerning the divine identity: the name (Ex), the power/authority (Mt); b) the orders regarding a specific divine mission, respectively to Moses (Ex) and to the disciples (Mt); c) and finally, the promise of the divine presence: "I am with you" (Ex) and "I am with you" (Mt).

FIRST SCENE

Moses: Ex 3:1–3   **The disciples:** Mt 28:16–17

— Moses arrives at the mountain of God	— the eleven go to the mountain indicated by Jesus
— I want to draw near and SEE...	— and when they SAW...
— Moses takes off his sandals	— the eleven prostrated themselves

SECOND SCENE

Yaweh speaks: Ex 3:4–12   **Jesus speaks:** Mt 28:18–20

a) revelation

"I am the God of your fathers..."	"All authority has been given to me"

b) mission/mandate

"Now go! I send you..."	"Go and make disciples..."

c) promise

"I am with you"	"I am with you"

For Matthew, the evangelist of the fulfillment, the disciples are the heirs of Moses, Israel's liberator from the oppression of Egypt and leader of the Exodus. With authority received from God, the Risen One confers on the disciples the mission for the new people of God and promises his assistance.

The journey of the eleven

The group of disciples is no longer the same. Jesus had constituted them according to the symbolic number of twelve, to represent all of Israel; now instead they are "the eleven."[4] The new designation reflects Judas' defection, but it also recalls that on the night of trial each of them failed.

The last encounter with the Master took place on that disconcerting night, when, panic-stricken, they all ran away, leaving him alone. Then, the day after the Sabbath, there came the incredible announcement of the women: the Master is alive and wants to meet them; he calls them "my brothers" and waits for them in Galilee! As they now remember he had predicted in his coming passion:

> "This night you will all lose your faith in me, for it is written: I will strike the shepherd, and the sheep of the flock will be scattered, but after I rise I will go ahead of you into Galilee" (26:31–32).

The conclusion therefore takes us back to the place where it all began, in Galilee of the pagans, where "the people living in darkness have seen a great light" (4:15).

If the eleven are again together, it is a sign that trust in the words of Jesus, who reunites them and sets them once more on the journey, triumphs over the bitter awareness of their prevailing sin (28:7, 10). They receive the invitation through the women, leaving Jerusalem and making their way to the place indicated. In so doing, they express their willingness to again take up their journey, walking behind the Lord. Following consists above all in obedience to the word.

---

4. Matthew is not worried about recomposing the number, as does Luke (cf. Acts 1:15–26).

Here we are on the mountain, the place of the disciples' paschal experience. Matthew sums up everything in three verbs: *they saw, they prostrated themselves, they doubted.*[5]

Attention is concentrated above all on "seeing" Jesus. There are no words, either in the form of a question or an exclamation. There is only contemplative silence, all eyes ecstatic. It is a "seeing" that brings one immediately to adoration: "Seeing him, they prostrated themselves." Before the glory of the Lord, the disciples find themselves, almost by instinct, in the attitude of reverence, their bodies folded in a profound bow. The solemn *proskynêsis* ("prostration") expresses complete recognition of and honor to the Risen Christ.[6] The women are described in the same attitude in Matthew 28:9, with the difference that they not only "prostrate themselves" (*proskyneô*), but also embrace his feet.

This scene of the eleven bowing before the *Kyrios*-Lord creates an effect of hieratic solemnity; it concretely brings to life the dimension of the Church's adoration before the Lord. The same attitude described the Magi coming from the East, when they entered the house and saw the baby with Mary, his mother: "They fell on their knees and worshiped him" (Mt 2:11). It also described the disciples on the night in which Jesus manifested himself to them as

---

5. The primary action, the "seeing," is expressed in a participle form that presupposes two successive reactions, both described as normal actions. The syntactic construction suggests the idea of contemporaneousness between the seeing and the adoring: and seeing him (*kài idòntes*), they prostrated themselves (*prosekynêsan*).

6. The *proskynêsis* is the profound bow which in the East substitutes for our genuflection.

Lord of creation, walking on the sea. At that time those
who were in the boat "worshiped him and said, 'Truly you
are the Son of God'" (Mt 14:33).

What surprises us here is that adoration exists alongside *doubt*. Although the eleven prostrate themselves
before his glory, they "doubted." How can the two things
exist together? Those who doubt are the same ones who
prostrate themselves: *hoi de edìstasan,* and the translation
"but some were doubtful" is in reality an attempt to sweet-
en the phrase. While the Christ who walked on water
caused the disciples to admire his divinity, the glory of the
Risen One now disconcerts them. Certainly it leads them
to adoration, but it does not remove their confusion. Even
though they recognize him, the disciples doubt. It isn't
because they do not believe, but their faith is weak; they
pass quickly from certainty to doubt (this is what the very
rare verb *distàzô* means). They are "men of little faith" like
Peter, who at first believes the word of the Master and
throws himself onto the water, but then very quickly is
overcome with fear and begins to sink while the Master
kindly reproves him: "O you of little faith, why did you
doubt?" (Mt 14:30–31, the only other time *distàzô* is
used!). In reality, doubt runs through the history of the
Church's faith, but it is conquered by the initiative of the
Risen One, who remains near.

The words of the Risen One

Jesus dominates the second scene. Here he imparts his
last words, and they have the sound of a solemn last will

and testament. But above all, his action stands out. The Risen Lord moves in the direction of his disciples: "he drew near them" (*prosélthôn*). Usually this verb describes the movement of the disciples, as in the appearance to Mary of Magdala and the other Mary: "they came forward [*prosélthousai*], took hold of his feet, and worshiped him" (28:9).[7] Only in one other passage does this verb have Jesus for its subject: on the mountain of the transfiguration, after he had manifested himself in his glory, he "drew near" to Peter, James, and John who had fallen to the earth on their faces.

It is like making contact again: first he draws near and then he speaks (Mt 17:7). The drawing near tends to establish communication and to reassure. The Risen One overcomes the distance that, as it pertains to the world of God, separates him from his disciples. Thus attention is concentrated on what remains: his word.

His last, brief discourse hinges on three passages, which offer a solemn declaration, a command, and a promise.

"All authority has been given to me"

The Risen One testifies first of all to his lordship: *all power* has been given to him, or rather the *fullness of authority* (*exousìa*). It is not as if he has automatically claimed this power or *stolen* it from God, as the tempter had insinuated (cf. Mt 4:9–10); rather, he has *received* it

---

7. In that context one says that Jesus "met up with" (*hypêntêsen*) the women. This does not take away the fact that the two protagonists "drew near" to him (Mt 28:9).

after having given everything. The passive formulation suggests that the Giver is God himself: "*All authority in heaven and on earth has been given* [i.e, by God] *to me.*" The Risen Jesus is the *Pantocrator;* he has received that fullness of authority that makes him the plenipotentiary of God. He has power also over death and hell.[8] His saving power has no limits and embraces heaven and earth.[9]

Make disciples of all nations

The discourse proceeds with a consequential "therefore" (*oun*). In the fullness of his power, the Risen One now expresses a command: "Go, therefore, and *make disciples* of all nations." The duty "to go" (the typical verb for sending) has as its objective not simply "to teach," as many versions translate it, but contains something much more demanding: discipleship. The disciples (*mathetài*) are sent to do what Jesus has done for them: *mathêtèusate,* "make-disciples."[10] This does not mean to "make proselytes," but rather to continue the journey begun by Jesus, to do what the Master of the meek and compassionate heart has done.

---

8. *Exousìa* describes of itself the whole ministry of Jesus, his teaching and his healing activity (cf. Mt 7:29; 8:9; 9:6, 8; 21:23, 24, 27); this is the saving power in which Jesus had also made his disciples participants, sending them to heal every kind of sickness (Mt 10:1). But now Jesus declares that he has received *pàsa exousìa,* that is to say, power of every kind and of the highest level, even over death.

9. The Messiah, "son of David," appears here clearly as David's Lord, constituted Son of God in power (Rom 1:3).

10. Beneath the syntactic profile, one observes that the command, formulated as the aorist imperative—*mathêtèusate*—is specified by three participles: first in the opening sentence "going," and then in two successive words that follow, "baptizing" and "teaching."

At this point all restrictions fall away. If at first the disciples were sent only to the lost sheep of the house of Israel (Mt 10:8), now they are sent to people of every race and culture.[11] With full authority the Risen One launches a universal mission and initiates the beginning of a new economy of salvation. "Disciples" of the Risen One will no longer become so through circumcision, as they did in the ancient covenant with Israel, but through the mediation of baptism in the name of the Holy Trinity; not simply by observing the Law of Moses but everything Jesus has taught.

It is decisively a new beginning! In his first discourse on the mountain, Jesus declared that he had come not to abolish the Law and the Prophets, but to bring them to fulfillment (5:17). And he added that not even an *iota* or a stroke of the Law would drop off without if being accomplished (5:17–18). So how is it that now what is being "dropped" is not just an iota, but precisely the great sign of the covenant made on the flesh of men, that is, circumcision? What happened to justify such a change? Have heaven and earth perhaps passed away?

Matthew seems to think so. He is the only evangelist who describes the death of Jesus as if it were the early arrival of the end of the world. Not only is this verified with an earthquake, as afterward on the morning of the resurrection, but tombs even open and the dead are raised;

---

11. In Matthew's view, Israel is not excluded as the audience for mission, but its refusal opens the door to the pagans.

they enter the holy city and appear to many (27:51–53). Without a doubt these are apocalyptic scenes meant to underscore the end of one epoch and the beginning of another. Precisely so: the heavens and the earth have passed away; one world has ended and another one is beginning, which justifies passing from the Law of Moses to the Gospel of Jesus, from circumcision (reserved only to men) to baptism (unreservedly open also to women). It is a passage that is neither abandonment nor substitution, but truly fulfillment. The foundation remains; the very God of the covenant renews in his Son the pact with humanity. "Neither circumcision nor uncircumcision is of any significance—a new creation is all that matters" (Gal 6:15), through faith in Jesus and baptism in the Holy Trinity.

"And behold, I will be with you all the days until the end of the age"

One is aware then of a change in tone; from the imperative we move to the indicative. And so the very last words are not a command but a consoling promise: "Behold, I am with you until the end of the world!" (Mt 28:20).

Unlike Luke, Matthew does not speak of the ascension into heaven (Lk 24:51; Acts 1:9–10), and so perpetuates the presence of the Risen One in his Church.[12] Jesus does not go away; he remains close to his disciples right to the

---

12. Luke sees Jesus blessing his disciples, yet detaching himself from his own and going up into heaven (Lk 24:51; Acts 1:9–10).

end of the world. His story reveals the marvelous reality of Emmanuel, the God-with-us![13]

Community in mission

The text we have meditated on has not depicted a holy or ideal community. On the contrary, it is a small and inadequate community that is sent on mission. Jesus called twelve disciples, with an evident allusion to the twelve tribes of Israel. Now they are eleven, and this simple fact reveals that the community is not victorious and perfect but inadequate; they did not hold up under the great trial of the passion. Jesus could have started over with others. Instead, he begins again with those he called and still considers "his brothers."

An inadequate and insufficient community, certainly, but one that is *put back on the journey,* a journey of hope, by the word of the Lord. They set off again from "Galilee of the Gentiles," where Jesus had begun his preaching of the Good News. The Lord is truly great; he does not make an appointment to meet them in Jerusalem, where they had failed, but in Galilee, where they had given the best of themselves when they had left everything to follow him, beginning with Simon and Andrew along the shores of Capernaum.

---

13. Now the full meaning of the name given by the angel to Joseph is revealed: "He will be called Emmanuel, which means God-with-us" (1:23).

From the "mountain" of Galilee, the disciples-church would "descend" and take up suffering of every kind, as Jesus had done before them, putting themselves at the service of the hope and joy of every human person.

BOOKS & MEDIA

The Daughters of St. Paul operate book and media centers at the following addresses. Visit, call or write the one nearest you today, or find us on the World Wide Web, www.pauline.org

CALIFORNIA
3908 Sepulveda Blvd, Culver City, CA 90230	310-397-8676
2650 Broadway Street, Redwood City, CA 94063	650-369-4230
5945 Balboa Avenue, San Diego, CA 92111	858-565-9181

FLORIDA
145 S.W. 107th Avenue, Miami, FL 33174	305-559-6715

HAWAII
1143 Bishop Street, Honolulu, HI 96813	808-521-2731
Neighbor Islands call:	866-521-2731

ILLINOIS
172 North Michigan Avenue, Chicago, IL 60601	312-346-4228

LOUISIANA
4403 Veterans Memorial Blvd, Metairie, LA 70006	504-887-7631

MASSACHUSETTS
885 Providence Hwy, Dedham, MA 02026	781-326-5385

MISSOURI
9804 Watson Road, St. Louis, MO 63126	314-965-3512

NEW JERSEY
561 U.S. Route 1, Wick Plaza, Edison, NJ 08817	732-572-1200

NEW YORK
150 East 52nd Street, New York, NY 10022	212-754-1110

PENNSYLVANIA
9171-A Roosevelt Blvd, Philadelphia, PA 19114	215-676-9494

SOUTH CAROLINA
243 King Street, Charleston, SC 29401	843-577-0175

TENNESSEE
4811 Poplar Avenue, Memphis, TN 38117	901-761-2987

TEXAS
114 Main Plaza, San Antonio, TX 78205	210-224-8101

VIRGINIA
1025 King Street, Alexandria, VA 22314	703-549-3806

CANADA
3022 Dufferin Street, Toronto, ON M6B 3T5	416-781-9131